ADVANCE PRAISE FOR *CRUSOE'S ISLAND*

"Heather Ross Miller stands out among all the North Carolina writers I know as inhabiting solid ground with her head in the planets. . . . In addition to being a memoir of her life, [*Crusoe's Island*] is a parable for ours: once upon a time, we were born, we grew up, we discovered words and wrote them down in notebooks. One day we read them aloud, and our difficult and ordinary lives became transformed into something profoundly mysterious, and we began understanding our story, as if for the first time . . . Superbly written, Heather's story will be clear to her readers, and our stories may begin to form in our own imaginations."—Emily Herring Wilson, author of *North Carolina Women: Making History*

"*Crusoe's Island* is an extraordinary novelesque memoir written by an award-winning poet and fiction writer in mid-career. [It's] a trip. Don't miss it."—Mary von S. Jarrell, author of *Remembering Randall: A Memoir of Poet, Critic, and Teacher Randall Jarrell*

PRAISE FOR *CHAMPEEN*
Published by Southern Methodist University Press, 1999

"A champeen of a novel . . . hilarious and poignant."—Bret Lott, author of *Jewel*

"A novel that hits all the right notes . . . funny, sad, and wholly satisfying."—Jill McCorkle, author of *Carolina Moon*

"I loved this book . . . I laughed and I cried and I was brought up short in the lovely way that only evidence of wisdom on the page can bring. Miller's voice is seductive . . . Throughout, I felt myself in the hands of a champeen storyteller."—Janet Peery, author of *The River Beyond the World*

"*Champeen* . . . is a lovely, bittersweet evocation of small-town life in North Carolina during World War II. I hated for it to end."—Lee Smith, author of *Fair and Tender Ladies*

CAROLINA WOMEN SERIES

CRUSOE'S ISLAND

BOOKS BY
HEATHER ROSS MILLER

Fiction

The Edge of the Woods
Tenants of the House
Gone a Hundred Miles
A Spiritual Divorce and Other Stories
In the Funny Papers
Champeen

Poetry

The Wind Southerly
Horse Horse, Tyger Tyger
Adam's First Wife
Hard Evidence
Friends and Assassins
Days of Love and Murder

Translations by Michel Gresset

L'Orée des bois, Editions Gallimard
De l'autre bout du monde, Editions Gallimard
La jupe espagnol, Mare Nostrum Editions

CRUSOE'S ISLAND

The Story of a Writer and a Place

HEATHER ROSS MILLER

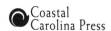

Published by
Coastal Carolina Press
4709 College Acres Drive, Suite 1
Wilmington, North Carolina 28403

Library of Congress Cataloging-in-Publication Data

Miller, Heather Ross, 1939–
    Crusoe's Island: the story of a writer and a place / Heather Ross
Miller.
        p. cm. (Carolina women series)
    ISBN 1–928556–04–3 (acid-free paper)
    1. Miller, Heather Ross, 1939—Homes and haunts—North Carolina.
    2. Authors, American—20th century—Family relationships. 3.
    Authors, American—20th century—Biography. 4. North Carolina—
    Social life and customs. 5. Miller, Heather Ross, 1939—Family. 6.
    Parks—North Carolina. I. Title. II. Series.

    PS3563.I38 Z465 2000
    818'. 5409—dc21
    [B]   00-029491

First edition

10 9 8 7 6 5 4 3 2 1

Acknowledgments

"Epilogue: Blue Moon" appeared in somewhat different form in *Pembroke Magazine*.

Lines from "The World as Meditation" by Wallace Stevens used by permission from Alfred A. Knopf.

I thank the Glenn Committee of Washington and Lee University whose generous grants enabled me to develop and finish this book.

I thank Emily Herring Wilson for her many critical readings.

As always, I thank Melissa and Kirk Miller, two good friends of mine, for their encouragement of my writing, and especially for their vivid memory of what went on in the park where they grew up.

Additional information can be found in:

State Parks of North Carolina, edited by Walter C. Biggs, Jr., and James F. Parnell. John F. Blair, Publisher, 1989.

Travels of William Bartram, edited by Mark Van Doren. Dover, 1955.

"The Candlewalk: A Midwinter Fire Festival," *North Carolina Folklore*, vol. 19, no. 4, November 1971.

"The Palmer Christian," *North Carolina Folklore*, vol. 24, no. 3, November 1976.

DISCLAIMER

Except for the family, names have been changed to protect privacy, and also to enhance the story-like atmosphere I wished to convey. These things did happen. But my telling about them happens in a place from which stories emerge. I hope a good place. Singletary Lake Group Camp exists. And so does Crusoe's Island.

Heather Ross Miller
July 1999

for
Melissa and Kirk
and
for the memory of
Clyde

Two in a deep-founded sheltering, friend and dear friend.

—Wallace Stevens
"The World As Meditation"

Contents

CRUSOE'S ISLAND

1
Real Beginnings

I ALWAYS START EVERY STORY calling the place Crusoe's Island. Not Singletary Lake Group Camp, an hour inland from the Atlantic. The real place where we lived for thirteen years. A place actually strange enough to mystify anybody. For me it has to be the wild and fictive Crusoe's Island, where terrors raged in the woods. And a woman got marooned.

Back to the real beginnings, before terrors, things in the stories assemble themselves in patterns both straight and strange. I need to do more than remember them all right, assemble them in order, for our children. For Clyde. I need the romance and sharp edge of Crusoe's Island.

Remembering back, a marriage can take on the fragrance of wild plums, persimmons, and blueberries. Accented by the hot dark flavor of strong coffee in mugs, a strong man's coffee. Not every man's taste. Not every woman's choice. Somewhere in there you have to look at the newspaper, or hear something on television, and then sweet things like plums and dark things like coffee go stale. A terror can set in. A terror of not remembering.

And not everybody would live in the woods, nor wish to be surrounded for thirteen years by such dense and secret places, places as remote, in some respects, as the moon. It took two people like us, Clyde and Heather.

The story opens:

Clyde Miller and Heather Ross met in a North Carolina state park called Morrow Mountain, in Stanly County, made out of thousands of acres of hardwoods and old pines, red clay and white quartz rock and boulders like the backs of huge wallowing hippopotamuses, gray and glistening. The Yadkin River spills off there into the Pee Dee, making Badin Lake at one end and Lake Tillery at the other.

Clyde was a park ranger. I was summer help, the park secretary, forty hours a week typing, filing, answering the phone. His job was the more exciting, wearing uniforms, driving around in a green state-owned truck, policing picnic areas and campsites and six rustic vacation cabins, protecting a valuable natural resource and, on a good day, getting to interpret that natural resource to park patrons.

We had grown up close to each other, but, separated by a generation, still didn't know each other. But when I got down to the park, I heard rumors about Clyde: he'd been in the navy, he'd been to Chapel Hill, to Mars Hill, to Bowling Green University, graduating finally from Pfeiffer College, the Methodist school just seventeen miles up the road. If you left your pocketbook in his way, the last summer's secretary warned me, Clyde Miller would paint right over it. He didn't care. He thrived on eccentricity. He lived in the kitchen of the ranger barracks, made it his pad, even had a hi-fi system built right into the kitchen cabinets. The other seasonal help, lifeguards and park attendants, boys between college semesters, were awed by the man, thirty years old, who filled the barracks with barbells and other weight-lifting equipment, papered the walls with *Playboy* centerfolds, and left cold bourbon in the fridge where even his own mother could see it.

They told me Clyde had slept with a hundred women.

And I, at nineteen, was tantalized.

He noticed me reading Joyce's *Dubliners*. I sat up in the park office one morning with my spanking clean Modern Library edition, all the weekly reports typed and sealed in an envelope to send to Raleigh, and Clyde came in wearing his official gray-green summer straw hat.

—I never saw anybody reading a book in here before, he said, not even taking off the hat.

I had already decided to be blunt and ornery. I turned two slow pages.

—Well, you have now, I said.

He grinned, removed the hat, and the next weekend, we went out in his impressive old car, a '37 Plymouth with a gray body and green trunk, fiery red wheels and no hubcaps. Clyde had the whole interior, seats and floor and ceiling, upholstered in a velvety gray plush. This was in 1959, when most people were tooling around in fins and purple taillights.

—Why don't you sit over here beside me? he said, driving with one hand, the other sprawled across the seat.

—Maybe I don't want to, I said. And he grinned again, as if he knew already how it would turn out, maybe, the rest of his natural life. And that set the tone for our July evening, full of pouring-down rain and sharp with contrasts, the streetlights reflecting off bright wet pavement and the blinking neon of the What-A-Burger drive-in. We sat at little parking slots and called in our order through little staticky phones. Clyde ordered a poached egg on whole wheat and hot tea. We watched the consternation going on behind the smeary plate glass window. A young man dashed out in the rain, holding his serving tray over his head. He said, Look, they ain't got no whole wheat, how about white bread? And they ain't got no hot tea, how about iced tea? And they ain't heard of no poached egg, how about a fried?

Clyde gazed at him, at the pelting rain. Very well, he said. I noted how this was his favorite pronouncement upon things. I giggled at the boy running back to the counter, giggled again at the fried egg that came sizzling on the plain toast. Clyde sent the boy back for hot sauce.

Following this, we went uptown and walked the wet streets and peered in storefronts, dime stores and hardware stores. At a corner newsstand, Clyde asked the man did he have any Jack Kerouac?

—Any Jack what? the man complained.

—Very well, said Clyde, and we resumed walking, then got in the old Plymouth and drove out to a skating rink called Gene and Hazel's, about five miles out in the county. We did not skate, just sat in there and consumed huge paper cups of bootleg beer and watched the other people whizzing around the gleaming hardwood floor. The whole place vibrated with the weight of those rollers, the wooden rink seemed to bounce, and I did not know Clyde was testing me, seeing how much of this I would take. Polite, and grinning, and gently putting me to the test.

—Say, I said, why'd you ask that man about Jack Kerouac?

Clyde shrugged. I wanted to see you read something else in the office.

—Well, look, I said, I already read Jack Kerouac.

—Very well.

And because I had never met anybody audacious enough to order a poached egg at a burger joint, and then ask for Jack

Kerouac at a small-town newsstand, before the evening was done, I got out on that rink and made a dozen smooth rounds with the clumsy rented skates, my red cotton sundress ballooning and showing off my tan. *I look good*, I told myself, *I look good*.

The next week those lifeguards and park attendants at Morrow Mountain were astonished, and reminded me, Hey, Clyde Miller's slept with a hundred women.

Clyde and I kept the old Plymouth for years. It took us to another park, Singletary Lake Group Camp, in coastal Bladen County, a place of white sand and turkey oaks, Spanish moss and cola-dark water.

Clyde Miller did everything in some quietly peculiar and specialized way, including marrying me about six months later in the dead of winter, a big snow on the ground, roads barely passable, Sunday, February 14, 1960. He drove the Plymouth to Greensboro where I was a junior at the Woman's College of the University of North Carolina, and I agreed to get married on Saturday, February 13, but the snow moved in, covered the whole state with a blinding silencing white. He had to leave the car in front of my dorm, trudge downtown to the Y to spend the night.

The next morning, Valentine's Day, the Plymouth, a smooth dune of snow, glittered as the sun came up over Greensboro. And I saw Clyde trudging back, hands in his pockets, cheeks red with cold and effort, trudging back to dig out the car and take me off to marry me.

My friends helped sweep the snow off the Plymouth, everybody shrieking and laughing, my happy wedding attendants in boots and toboggans: Roseanne, Carrie Beth, Dottie, and Jo, my friends and neighbors in Ragsdale Dorm. They stood knee-deep

Author with cat, 1968

in that splendid and exasperating snow, breathless, excited, gave us a shove and a cheer and we drove off slowly, the chains grinding, finding at last a purchase on the pavement.

We got married at Wesley Chapel, a small Methodist church in the countryside close to Pfeiffer College. Clyde wanted to be married by Dr. Scheele, his favorite professor, a sociologist and an ordained minister. At Wesley Chapel, old and wooden, its paint as white as the new snow in the sun, Clyde found two people to witness the marriage. They sat in the front pews and watched and smiled as Dr. Scheele began, and Clyde and I stood there and said the words that married us for life.

I would come to discover later how much family history was associated with Wesley Chapel, that the old Millers, Clyde's long-ago ancestors, first settled in the area around the church, then slowly migrated southward to the valley around Morrow Mountain, eventually building what was known as Miller Town. An adventurous people. But that Sunday afternoon, all I knew was the cozy welcoming air of the church, the encouragement of Dr. Scheele, and the snow spreading away into the horizon outside.

When it was done, we drove the Plymouth down to Morrow Mountain State Park, through deeper snow, shadows stretching long and bluish across the winding road. We drove straight to our friend, Pollard, the superintendent.

Before we went in the house, before we even got very far into the park, inching along the snow, Clyde asked, Can you live this? He took one hand from the wheel and motioned at the thick woods crowding the road, crusted and bowed with the snow.

I gazed at the heavy trees, the long blue shadows ringing across the snow. I could smell the blue shadows and the deep snow. And I nodded my head, patted his hand. Our hands were freezing. We had new gold rings from Schiffman's in Greensboro. Clyde took my cold hand, kissed it.

Then we went into Pollard's cozy house, where he and his family toasted Clyde and me with many little glasses of red wine, a bright fire crackling on the hearth, Pollard's two children tumbling around like pups.

The next summer I had graduated from college, and we were driving home from Greensboro in a hot June night, and somewhere through the Uwharrie hills, we saw thousands of lightning bugs all over the woods and fields. Lightning bugs hanging to the eaves of roofs, ringing fence posts, glowing over trees and smashing into the hood and windshield of the old Plymouth. A festival of living lights. Clyde and I were surprised the things stuck on so stubbornly, dotting the radio aerial, then blowing off into the dark like sparklers. Clyde said we could be driving through a galaxy, going into another dimension.

Within another three months, we did. Clyde got transferred to Singletary Lake Group Camp, charged with the administration and protection not only of Singletary, but of all the Carolina bay lakes in the area. It was a deliberate move, something we embraced and welcomed, and so we packed up our year-old baby girl, Melissa, and went.

We were required to live in the park in a house provided by the state and to pay rent on it. That house, along with the other buildings, boats and machinery, trucks, and miscellaneous park equipment, down to the last ten-penny nail, appeared on the last official inventory. It was a statistic.

A big redwood gate had to be locked and unlocked at the park entrance. And a rustic redwood sign set at an angle in our white sandy front yard read *Superintendent's Residence* in deeply carved letters, highlighted ocher against the wood. The rangers carved out those signs during the winter, what is called the off-season, when there was less outside work. All over the park, those deep letters proclaimed *Group Use, No Parking, Official Vehicles Only*.

Thus, it was never our house in the regular sense, with deed and title, a plat book registry. But Clyde and I would make it ours. Rebuilding it, maybe, with feelings and energies, the timbers rising up, the ridge pole and shingles, maybe never quite finished, and already exuding a sweet gum in the hot noon sun, the way Thoreau said his house did out there in the woods beside Walden Pond. I liked the idea of gum oozing from our Bladen County timbers, its pungency and its clear amber color. I liked it sticking to my own fingers. I wasn't Thoreau's wife, though. I was a woman in the middle of a state park in North Carolina. And I was married to Clyde Miller, a man who was as self-sufficient and contained as Thoreau, happy to be in the woods away from noise and glamour.

We walked out to the big flat deserted lake and heard wild ducks and geese honking somewhere on the far shore. Out in the middle, the birds moved like hundreds of dark spots, settling and resettling. Their delicate fluff and pale feathers floated along the pier pilings, caught in pondweed and juniper. The clean fragrance of longleaf pines hung over everything. Warm enough to be spring, the air so soft it stroked my face. Yet it was late December, almost Christmas, 1961. The baby grabbed at things in the white sand, sticks and long brown pine straw, an old gray seashell. It seemed all right there. It smelled good.

And Clyde asked me, as he had back in the Piedmont on our snowy wedding day, Do you think you can stand this? His voice patiently questioning, his eyes a curious blue.

Sure, I said, sure I can. And we walked home, swinging the baby between us. His woodsy, sweaty smell comforted me, a smell streaking through his gray uniform shirt, something tangible that put a skin on our adventures just beginning.

We got there a few days before Christmas. The Plymouth broke down in Wadesboro, where the Piedmont begins to drop and flatten into the Carolina sand hills and peach orchards. We spent a few hours in some repair garage, Melissa running all over the pavement, Clyde holding her by the pink straps of her corduroy overalls, Zoom, zoom, zoom! Run, run, run!, he encouraged her, while I sat inside reading the papers and drinking coffee.

This meant the movers got to Singletary ahead of us and had already unloaded our little assortment of belongings and placed them about the house according to their own imaginations. A second-hand white-painted baby crib, a second-hand four-poster bed, a second-hand electric range and refrigerator, boxes of books and shoes, and the Betsy Ross spinet I practiced on. My mother once hoped I might turn into a passable piano player.

—Take it, she had said, it'll help fill up a wall.

One of the movers, amused by this mismatched stuff, observed, Well, you all ain't got much. But at least it's you all's.

He was righter than he knew. Clyde and I were in the middle of the woods, poor and educated, stoic and sensitive, full of great ideas but with little capital. There were few things among that assortment we had actually paid money for. Old splint-bottom chairs found in an attic, a slant-topped desk rescued from a hayloft: These made up our accouterments. And the elegant Betsy Ross spinet.

After unhooking the cab from the van, the movers went off to Elizabethtown for the evening. Later in the night, they returned to sleep in the van still parked right up to the front door, almost on the front porch. Clyde and I could hear them belch and fart until morning.

Melissa woke up in her strange new room and her cry echoed through the house. We didn't have enough stuff to absorb a baby's crying. Our few things scattered in the house only seemed to define its emptiness.

But already it was becoming ours. The big rooms with their heavy walls of real panels in dark knotty pine, the impressive brick fireplace that filled one wall in the long living-room with two exposed beams, the little kitchen, the attic and porch. I picked up the baby and walked through these rooms with her, looking out of every new window at the sand gleaming white in the moon, at the thick woods crowding in on us from every direction. In the kitchen, a drop of water from the faucet glittered, hung a moment like a long tear, then fell with a soft plop.

It comforted me and Melissa both to hear that. A dripping kitchen sink in the middle of all those woods, in the middle of all that gleaming moonlit sand. I hugged the baby tighter. It was a very dark house, accented by moonlight. In the morning, we would look for Christmas greens, festoon this dark moonlit place with pine and cedar, prickly holly wreaths.

Next day, we walked across our white sandy yard and into the longleaf pines behind the house. Melissa watched me fill a paper bag with big prickly cones. Some of the cones looked to be ten inches long, each one fragrant and rough. I gave her a pine tuft to drag through the sand and she ran around as she had the day before, running all over that garage in Wadesboro. Suddenly, service stations and garages seemed far off and almost unreal to me in such thick piney-woods isolation.

When I picked her up, the baby smelled of resin and pine straw, a wonderful pungency mixed with her own of baby shampoo and talcum. Those were good smells, healthy and restorative and reassuring. I took a deep hungry breath and squeezed her. This whole place, I thought, will turn into linked moments of smells, Clyde, Melissa, myself, pines, sand, dark lake water.

Coming back toward the house, I discovered geoasters spread around like dark gray dried-up stars. Curious little fungi, that was their name: stars of the earth, earth stars.

—Looky here, I said, stars.

Melissa hunkered down with me. And we poked them all open with our Christmas pine. Thin brown soot fell out and blew off. The five petals of the stars looked like claws bulging out of the sand around a center globe, then curving back under. Like mushrooms split open in some kind of ecstasy and then fixed that way. Froze, maybe, the way my mother used to warn I would if I made faces. Don't make that ugly face. You'll freeze that way.

The sooty spores reminded me of old thin snuff as I dotted some on a finger and sniffed. Melissa did the same, dotting her nose. Geoasters smelled like the sand, cold and dry and with a faint undertone of rot, dried-up mushrooms, dull and harmless.

My grandmother on my mother's side, Grandmother Martha Anna Smith, dipped snuff, Railroad Mills Sweet, keeping a fresh supply of toothbrushes on the mantel. Little sassafras twigs she found in the woods around her farm. She'd dipped snuff since she was four years old when her older sisters, those girls born before the Civil War, showed her how.

I thought of her now in these woods, the turkey oaks and Spanish moss and sand so different from woods she knew. The huge pine cones in my paper bag. I thought, well, look at my little girl down in the sand exploring geoasters. My Grandmother Martha Anna was always a lonely woman after her husband shot himself, seeking a far corner of woods, the shotgun like a clumsy crutch. My mother only sixteen.

Somehow the visions all boiled down to a sooty handful of snuff dust here.

I told Melissa maybe we could spray-paint the geoasters gold and silver and put them on the Christmas tree. Then, I told her, they might look like little gold and silver claws.

—Claws, Melissa said solemnly and kept worrying at the sooty geoasters until she sneezed and we went inside and I looked them up in a book. Those in the backyard were *Geoaster nanus*, common to sandy regions and sea dunes. The sooty stuff, the book assured me, was of no alimentary interest.

I wiped it off the baby's face, anyhow.

We put the longleaf pine across the brick mantelpiece and though it was still unseasonably warm, Clyde built a bright fire for Christmas Eve. Then we put out the toys for Melissa, a white Persian cat with a music box in its belly and eyes as blue as jewels, a yellow Tonka truck, a rocking chair, and a red wagon.

I went to look at Melissa sleeping in her room paneled the same dark knotty pine as the rest of the house. One arm poked through the crib bars. Her head was a damp tangle of curls, and her eyelids, thin as paper, moved with her dreams.

I liked all that, the dark whorls and streaks of the pine panels, the baby sound asleep, and the place deep in the middle of coastal woodlands. I drank it in, wrapped it around me like a shawl, then went back to sit with Clyde in front of the Christmas fire. He mixed coffee and bourbon, what he called coffee royal, and I thought nothing would ever match that moment, that place, the rich smells now of coffee and the crackling fire, a mug warming my hands, then the tang of the rich bourbon across my tongue.

No sad grandfather out in these woods with his shotgun, no lonely old woman with nothing left but snuff and sassafras in her apron. Clyde and I would have love and strength in one small place. A bright fire, a sleeping baby, and each other. And so I would minister to Clyde and he to me, and so we would make love on the rug in front of the fire, and so we would give comfort.

And later in bed, through the long Christmas Eve, isolated and unique, we would lie awake talking quietly, as was our custom, and listening to the sounds of the night.

2
The Wind Theory

O UR HOUSE STOOD FIFTY MILES round-trip from Elizabethtown, a distance I had to get used to traveling every
week. Fifty miles through scrub and turkey oaks, the tall pines, the
gray moss like swinging squirrels' tails. There were two trees I used
for counters, and I quickly taught Melissa to watch for them when
she got restless in her aqua vinyl car seat, bored with flipping the
colored spools decorating its frame.

—See, look! See the bird tree?

One tree, an old hollow pole drilled full of holes, its limbs like
polished bones for birds to perch on. It stood in a spreading field
of thick broom straw that caught the setting sun and turned fiery
red, so red the field always startled me coming upon it in the car,
anxious to reach the park before nightfall.

—Bud tree, said Melissa solemnly, bud.

The other, an old oak struck by lightning and twisted in dark
shapes seemed to me like some monster trying to break loose. No

birds perching there, it rose high enough to challenge the pines and defy the flat horizon. That one I called the scary tree. I wondered if I should say *scary* to Melissa. Wondered if the baby realized the impact of the names, but she did recognize the trees going into town, coming back from town, and I liked to hear her identifying them, pointing a wet finger, bud tree, bud tree, Mama! Then a bit further, sca'ee tree, Mama! Not many r's in her mouth yet. Somehow that soft, rolled syllable made the trees even more special to me, more birdlike, and even more scary. I always reached to pat Melissa when we passed that tree.

Clyde and I named other landmarks and paced off the boundaries of our isolation, and so came to cherish it all for our own. Singletary, part of the Carolina bay lakes, had been acquired by the state from the federal government in 1936, the year my parents got married, and three years before I was born. The facts about Singletary could be read in any state park brochure. The facts of my life just beginning there in late 1961, in the turning of the year, were clothed and fed in the skin and smell and heartbeat of three people, a man and a woman, their baby. Not just my parents and me, but my husband, my daughter, and me, Heather Miller. And Clyde's parents and himself. These very real, sometimes peculiar, more oftentimes ordinary people put a skin to Singletary Lake Group Camp, a distinguishing smell, a steady heartbeat.

But the original three, Clyde and me and our daughter, we were the reasons I called it Crusoe's Island. I thought about Robinson, the hairy man with the umbrella and the goats, about his man Friday, the islander saved from the stewpot. I thought about Carolina islands, being marooned, being all alone in the middle of nothing, a sea of trees, a desert of pine needles and sand and Spanish moss. This both tantalized and worried me.

So I called it Crusoe's Island.

When the lake level was down, there actually was a small mound toward the north side, about ten feet offshore. You could

The Scary Tree

call it an island. But there was no shipwrecked man there, no native, no footprints from cannibals. Just scrub and sand, a few tall junipers usually half-covered by flat dark water. And no way to get to it except by boat.

Clyde was often gone now, learning the dimensions of his new job, traveling the boundaries of Singletary Lake Group Camp and Bladen Lakes State Forest, meeting people, feeling out the place. But he found time to explore with me and Melissa the park lands closest to us, those areas that surrounded our house, connected by strips of trees and banks of sand, a circle of paved road.

Just down that road was the group camp where one hundred persons could gather at a time to occupy the primitive log cabins, taking showers in wash houses with skylights actually open to the sun and moon. They lined up for meals in the mess hall. The fireplace spread across one entire wall of the timbered dining room. Since it was Christmas, then New Year's when we first got there, I coveted that big fireplace and even crept inside it, crouching down between the huge andirons and peering up the chimney. Melissa followed, straddled the andirons, got smut on her hands and her red parka hood.

—Now you know how Santa Claus feels, said Clyde.

—Do they really use this fireplace? I knew they did. I was standing in a thin layer of ashes.

—Sometimes. Too much trouble, though, to get a big fire going in there. Clyde was leaving me, going into the kitchen. It's just for show, I think.

If I had that big fireplace, I told myself, I'd keep a fire going there all the time. Cook on it, too, with pots bubbling and skillets crackling. I'd haul in a Yule log and burn it until the last frost melted in the spring

The kitchen held other fascinations. A butcher's block commanded the center of it, a smooth hollow in the top worn from many slow slaps of the blade. Big sinks with old-fashioned drainboards and high-seated faucets with enamel labels Hot and Cold. The walk-in cooler, door thick as a tree, dark and peaceful, smelled a little mossy. I wanted all those things, too, as well as the huge wall fireplace. I thought of family dinners I would cook and serve, inviting all the friends and relations, Millers, Rosses, people up and down the road here, Kelly Star Route. My paternal grand-mother, Jennie Ross, whose husband did not shoot himself, whose sisters, instead of giving her snuff, giggled secrets about sex while embroidering fancy shirtwaists, this grandmother was a woman who thrived on cooking big family dinners. She even had a serv-ing window cut between her kitchen and dining room, a smaller version of what was here in this big mess hall. A jolly, generous woman, she cooked up chicken and dressing, apple-and-custard pies, and at Christmas, exotic coconut-orange ambrosia, passing it all through the little window to children and neighbors, the steam causing her long hair to slip its pins, curl slightly. Jennie had a strength and generosity I wanted to cultivate in my own house.

My daydreams ran away with my colorful grandmother and her generous succulent roast chickens. I wondered if we could withstand a siege in this place, hold off armies, our cooler stocked, our faucets running with clear plentiful water, and our hearth burning Yule logs. A castle made of chink and shingles, pines and turkey oaks, Spanish moss, white sand.

Outside the mess hall, oak leaves piled against the wide wooden steps suddenly took the wind, tossing and scattering across the group camp, flailing the nailed-down screens like long dry claws.

—Come on! I called to Melissa and together we chased the leaves, grabbing handfuls and throwing them.

And then around one little cabin, what Clyde called the craft shop, I found thousands of little colored beads and scraps of braided vinyl lanyards. I bent to scoop them, red and blue and black. They seemed to glitter in the dull white sand. Each bead with a tiny hole.

—They should've cleaned that up, said Clyde, they should've policed this area better. No real criticism in his voice, just point-ing out his ubiquitous state park policy.

I was glad they didn't clean it all up, had left the little beads and braids half-buried in sand and leaves for me and the baby to find with such glee. I collected enough beads to string a necklace. Melissa stuffed the lanyards in her corduroy pockets, still smutty from the mess hall fireplace and irons. And Clyde was amused at us both, scavenging away in the sand and turkey oaks.

He liked things to be cleaned up and squared away, a result of his navy years. But he also liked spontaneity, the way Melissa and I grubbed up the colored beads and planned the little pieces of jewelry.

There was plenty to scavenge in a place you could call Crusoe's Island. And things to stumble across in our explorations. Long before the state took it over, the Federal Resettlement Administration had set up peeled-pole picnic shelters, water fountains, and brick barbecue grills around one side of the lake. But the shelters and grills were too close to the shoreline in some places and on too swampy a foundation in others. By the time Clyde and I got there, they had grown over in wild grapevines and pond bay, tightened by honeysuckle and bamboo briar.

That first week, though, wandering around between Christmas and New Year's, the weather warm and gentle as May, we didn't know such history yet. I saw what I thought were ruins, a pitched shed roof in the brush, then a pile of mossy bricks with a grill set in its midst, and most marvelous of all, an old steel water bubbler lying in the spongy bracken.

Looky! I plunged ahead of Clyde and the baby, thinking about snakes and black bears and old witchy-women in gingerbread houses, but wanting to discover things despite them. To get my bearings. Stake a claim.

—It's like a fort, I said, a rampart, and poked at the peeled poles. They still held together in a pitched shed roof, the old shingles flaking off. Conjuring up for me rough palisades, hermits marooned for years, castaways and pirates and sleeping beauties under a spell.

Melissa inspected the brick barbecue built like a little chimney, the way people used to build such things before the advent of charcoal briquettes and rotisseries. She scooped a fistful of acorns, then threw them all at once, her short fingers spreading out.

—Why don't they fix these things up? I asked, use them again?

Clyde pressed a boot into the ground and stepped away. That's why. His footprint immediately filled with dark water glistening in the December sun.

I watched Clyde's footprint fill, then pressed my own into the spongy ground. It filled as quickly as his. Oh, I see, I see.

—Couldn't take the use, said Clyde. The wrong place for a picnic area. Everybody sinking into the swamp.

But something about my footprint and Clyde's filling with water and vanishing into the undergrowth of Singletary thrilled me. Maybe, I thought, it's what some people really want, to disappear from view, yet make a print—so deep down in the ground their footprints are still there. Maybe it's what I want.

Crusoe was on his island fifteen long years before he found the first footprint. Several more years before he found Friday. How many years before I found a footprint that filled and stayed?

Such physical demonstrations made me eager for more. This place was going to affect me and Clyde and Melissa. I could already tell. So I began looking up things about the park, the bay lakes. I suddenly wanted to know how things got there in the first place. Clyde had two geology books left over from his days at Chapel Hill, physical and historical geology. I dug them out of the packing boxes one evening, displacing bushels of old shoes in the process. It seemed we owned books and old shoes in excess, and the movers had boxed up both together.

After first sitting on the floor and trying on a pair of hideous old red thong sandals, I moved to the studio bed that served us as a sofa and opened the two geology texts. I found the Carolina bays and basins mentioned in both. Clyde liked me delving in those old texts, brought me cups of coffee and settled close by with other books. We could do things like that, settling close and reading, sipping coffee, and feel a strong, if simple, bond emerge. A thing of value. Not valued by everyone, maybe, but surely valued by us. Especially in the middle of those woods. Those Carolina bays, where we had only each other.

I thumbed through the geology books and studied the fading illustrations (noting also how many girls' names and telephone numbers Clyde Miller had scrawled in the margins). And I learned that the gigantic Pleistocene glaciers never covered the Carolinas, so these southern ovals, of which Crusoe's Island was one, were not formed the way most lakes in the northern hemisphere were, by big ice sheets melting and shrinking and scratching out lake beds, throwing around boulders and drifting and clawing the top of the continent.

No, the Carolina bay lakes were formed, these textbooks conjectured, by ancient meteors striking the earth and scooping out shallow bowls that filled up over the years from rain or ground water percolating from the adjoining swamps.

I liked that verb, *percolating.* It sounded so cozy and congenial, like the good dark mug of coffee my husband brewed for me, his specialty. And I lay back, savoring the coffee, and imagining the meteors plummeting toward this place to scoop out the shallow bowl called Singletary. I slapped my red thongs on the floor, turned another page.

Other scientists, the book continued, believed the bays were the remnants of ancient seas, the receding salt water slowly replaced by fresh mineral water strong enough to put a tang in your mouth and a dark stain on your clothes. And still others maintained the wind struck like mighty fingers across a mighty harp, rippling and sifting the earth, leaving many shallow depressions to fill with rain or swamp runoff. The Aeolian effect, that one was called.

I began to favor the wind theory, the Aeolian effect, and thought how those fingers scooped back and laid open the earth here, hollowed it out and ridged it finally in dunes and pines and turkey oaks, veiling it in that gray romantic epiphyte, the Spanish moss. Maiden's hair, the Indians called it, long and soft as a whisper, falling through the trees, pulling nutrients from thin air, a cousin of the pineapple.

—What are you thinking about? Clyde nudged me, glancing over the pages where he'd underlined things, chapter headings, notes to remind himself about lab quizzes.

—Spanish moss, I said, and the wind, what they call the Aeolian effect, to make the bay lakes. I sat up, stretched.

Clyde considered a moment, then, If you go look at the sand, he said, you can see why they believe that. It's just exactly the way the wind blows the sand, ripples it, scoops it up.

I wanted to go outside right then and look at the sand. Then I remembered it was already dark and I had on those red thongs. I'll go look at it tomorrow, I said. I'll look at it all over the park.

The Aeolian effect meant the wind just took over and left us a big section of coastal Carolina dotted with those elliptical things running parallel to each other northwest by southeast. Hundreds of exciting craters for me to run upon, lay claim to.

Clyde picked up my foot in the red sandal and stroked the skin of my instep. I like you in these, he said, especially if you paint your toenails the same color of red.

Heather with Melissa, December 1961

—I hate these old ugly things, I said, but I was pleased he liked them on me, and wondered where I might get nail polish in the woods.

The next day came colder, driving down the freak spring we had, pushing it back into those elliptical bays and burying it under thick brown leaves. A true January. I bundled the baby and went looking at the Aeolian effect in the sand. And exactly as Clyde had promised, the little ridges and streaks stretched all over making miniature dunes, Saharas, Gobis, the savannas of the moon. They felt cold to my touch as I pushed at the configurations with my toe and the polished nail gleamed. I had actually found some red polish in a jumble of lipsticks and eyeliners, and kept on the thongs to show it off.

An aerial photograph in Clyde's park office showed me those craters clearly. They resembled the pits and pocks of the moon, all shallow, some filled with dark water, others grown up in trees, but all of them very definitely a hundred or more miles from the Atlantic, all around them, crowding them. I touched a finger to each one, traced their rims.

The photograph was an old one, enlarged and printed onto poster board, framed in narrow pine strips. No glass. Somebody had printed small white letters: *Bay Lakes, 1949.*

Clyde stayed busy on the park phone, arranging the park schedules, making work plans. Melissa rummaged in the lower drawer of the file cabinet, throwing out pencils, manila folders, old tape measures, a bird's nest. But I kept on fantasizing about the Aeolian effect, sitting on the side of Clyde's desk, staring at the big photograph.

The craters lay a long time unseen, except for birds and animals, their sandy rims slowly eroding to form narrow exposed beaches at the southeast shore. The hard-pan clay of the lake beds gradually lined with sand and as trees and other vegetation began to flourish around the bays, peat developed toward the centers. Singletary right now had a pulpy peat bottom under its dark cola water and eventually it would fill in. Just like our footprints.

I blinked, shivered, regretting the thong sandals, my half-naked feet. I felt wind blowing over me. I felt I was the lake out there being caressed and coaxed.

One of the rangers came through the door, hailing us loudly, letting in the cold air. Melissa stopped her rummaging to stare at this new man. And Clyde got off the phone and began to show him the schedules.

I collected myself, guided the baby toward the door. And once outside, the stiff January wind buffeted us like boxing gloves. Nothing stopped the wind. The wind buffeted and pushed, forced more and more dark sediment down through the lake water.

Whole forests would grow where Singletary Lake now stood. People would walk on water.

It dizzied me, like looking at those quirky *Life* magazine covers where somebody is looking into a mirror into a mirror into another mirror. Infinity. An endless reflection of meteors and darkly percolating water, swamp runoff, juniper bushes, oval bays, and cold bone-white sand.

All the lakes around me in early 1962 brimmed with shallow cola water, perhaps 13 to 15 feet at their deepest parts. They had names like Black Lake, Lake Waccamaw, Jones Lake, Salter's Lake, Sugg's Mill Pond, and one, crystal clear, called White Lake.

Over the next months, I came to know certain things. The prevailing winds were from the west. The deepest parts of this Crusoe were at the southeast shore, and this held true for all the other lakes as well. Its swamps were thick and mysterious and deadly, populated by alligators and water moccasins, as well as deer, foxes, bobcats, and black bears. The woods were always strikingly dark and fragrant against the sand, enhanced by the Spanish moss and abundant blueberry bogs.

I came to know Crusoe was not a place for everybody. A person from Raleigh or Charlotte might well go a little crazy there in the silence and the solitude of those trees, that whispering sand. Suspicious of the thick peace gliding in every evening over the tops of pines and oaks, pouring like breath through the low scrub.

A person might well curse this isolation as beautiful and remote as the moon, and hurry back to her bustling, impersonal traffic, her solid pavement impervious to any Aeolian effect, and hide beneath the piquant smell of crowds.

3
Fire and Water

IN MARCH, FORESTRY LOOKOUTS in Lagoon Tower spotted smoke across Kelly Star Route. We were in the middle of supper when the call came. Clyde put me and Melissa in the black patrol car with the big whip antenna and shortwave, and we drove around looking for flames. The thick night sky overhead, the thick woods on either side—rather than closing in on us seemed to open out and sweep away, bringing a sense of horizon. And the patrol car with its lighted dials and radio static took us like a spaceship into the depths of Crusoe woods. Clyde still in his uniform, the baby nodding in my lap, I felt excited to be in on this adventure.

We found the fire on the other side of the highway, crackling behind some turkey oaks and pines. A little settlement there, sheds, pens, and some old houses rambling apart from their tin roofs, the front porches sagging. Three black women sat on the steps of one house watching the brush fire roar in their bare yard.

Nobody else around and no other lights or fires. A truck sat on blocks, its hood lifted like a jaw.

We drove up closer and Clyde got out. I stayed in the car with Melissa who was now sleeping, making little wet snores on my neck. Good evening, he said to the three women. I could hear everything through his open window.

They nodded, sizing the white people up. Clyde wanted to know why they were burning such a big fire out there without any help. It's too dry, he said, we're in a no-burn season right now. Anything wrong? Do you need some help?

One of them took a snuff brush out of her mouth, swabbed it into a can, and packed it back neatly in her lip. She wiped her hands on her knees.

—We seen a snake in there, she said. He crawl up in that brush pile.

The two other women chuckled, wiped their hands on their knees, too, and smoothed their hair. The fire gave their faces a magnificent gleam. Clyde talked a while longer. They all laughed, seemed to ease up. Then the one with the snuff brush rose from her step and came across the yard, skirting the roaring brush, to peer at me and the baby. She gazed, then said as if proclaiming a benediction, That a good-lookin baby. Bent closer, added, With a bunch of hair on its head.

I was flattered, smiling and eager to agree with her, but before I could say anything, the woman asked, That a boy or a girl?

—A girl. I shifted so she could see Melissa's face better in the firelight. Melissa's lips pulsed open and shut with her soft snores. Her cheeks flushed, her hair like a cloud.

The old woman, small and wizened as my Grandmother Martha Anna Smith, proclaimed once more. Boys you treats mean as you likes. But when it comes to lovin, ain't nothin like a girl.

Then she turned and went back to her step, dismissing us like some kind of curiosity.

Clyde dug them a trench around the brush. Don't go to bed and leave this fire still burning out here, he said. Wait till it dies down good and then put some dirt on it.

They mumbled something agreeable.

Clyde drove off, and I was still dazzled. *But when it comes to lovin, ain't nothin like a girl.*

That spring, fires burned along the middle southeastern seaboard, in the Great Dismal Swamp, disturbing the bottom lands and floodplains, stretching into the northern counties of eastern North Carolina and threatening, eventually, those of us in the far southern counties.

For days a thick haze hung in the sky, remnants of the smoke. That was the most frightening to me. I went outside with the baby in my arms and looked for the sun behind it. Just a thin flashing disk. Like something stuck up there. Something glued. Something fading away, or being swallowed alive by hungry animals.

The weak sun alarmed me. I felt deserted by nature. I realized I had been taking the sun for granted all my life. That I'd never really missed it before.

Clyde told me a spring fire was worse than a fall or winter fire. It destroyed all the new growth. A fall or winter fire just burned over the dormant trees. Life slept through the whole thing and woke up in the new year already tested and toughened.

But any kind of fire, spring or winter, was terrible to wait for, live through, witness. That spring we only waited for it to come. The haze from its smoke hanging over our woods and roof in a big dirty oily cloud. It stuck to my face and arms and when Melissa, who had fallen asleep in my arms, woke up, she had little white crescents under each eye. The stuff settled on her lashes.

Singletary Lake Group Camp rangers worked with Bladen Lakes state foresters, getting ready for the fire should the winds shift and blow it down on us in full conflagration. They bulldozed trenches and hosed down brushy thickets. They equipped the bombers to drop chemicals and water. They pumped up their Indian Pack fire extinguishers. And everybody got jumpy as the days went by and there was nothing to look at but the smoke.

My eyes stung from it. I pulled my fingers across the front door and left long gray smears behind. Melissa did it, too. I drew a stick man and woman and little girl, then a stick dog and cat. Wrote *Melissa* in the goo. We made hand prints, giggling. Then I got a bunch of paper towels and we scoured it off together.

One day we smelled the fire, the smoke and haze taking on a more acrid and gritty quality. And Clyde began taking us when he went on park patrol both morning and evening, Melissa sitting in my lap, her face as smudgy as ours. I felt again as I had the night we went across Kelly Star Route and found the three black women burning up a snake in their brush pile. Felt privileged to be let in on the adventure. A sense of wide horizon.

But it wasn't a joke. I never felt it was a joke. And this time, the fantastic quality of the adventure turned somber. Back in March, I had compared the patrol car to a spaceship plunging us into the depths of Crusoe woods. Now I just wanted it to work and get us out of there.

Yet I also felt a curious elation and curiosity. I was looking forward to the fire, to the thrill of it despite the danger, to the bombers and the bulldozers, to fighting a powerful element, fire. How would I fight it? Escape it? I wondered. With wind and earth? And with water?

That night I washed the smudge off the baby, washed out the tub, then filled it up again, just in case. I filled up a bucket, the kettle, two dishpans, filled up the kitchen sink. I was filling plastic jugs when Clyde came in.

—What's all this? He inspected the dripping faucets, my buckets and kettle and two dishpans slopping over the floor.

—This is to fight the fire with, I said, even though I knew how useless that assembly of water would be. In case the house catches, I gestured, in case we get trapped and you're gone off, I'll have some water to fight it with. I'll get in the tub, with Melissa.

He studied me a moment. If the house catches, he said, I won't be gone off. I'll move you and Melissa far away from here.

Clyde put a hand on either side of me. He looked me deep in the eye. His eyes blue and rich and serious. Anybody goes off, he declared, we'll go off together.

I took in the whole presence of him, his familiar smells of forest and clean sweat and health. And although Clyde delighted me, thrilled me to the core with his concern for me and Melissa, and his simple sensible plan, he also caused me some envy. I had been going about it in some crazy way, filling up bathtubs and kettles to fight a forest fire, not really thinking. Clyde had already made plans to evacuate us all. He wouldn't waste time fighting fire hand to hand around there or huddling in a ridiculous bathtub. He'd move us early, take us far away. Let the bombers and the bulldozers fight it.

He was right. I had underestimated him.

I always liked to watch other people underestimate Clyde, his soft-spoken manner, a man never given to display. He would stand listening to some lofty conversation, then just as these people had spent their opinions, he would utter a few quiet words, turn on a heel, and leave them blinking.

It would be hard to show such a man on the page. His friendly quietness might almost erase him. He entered the United States Navy at seventeen. Was nineteen, a gunner's mate first class aboard the USS *West Virginia* when Pearl Harbor exploded around him one ordinary Hawaiian Sunday morning. I was about two years old then, on the other side of the world, back in Badin. My parents and I had gone down to visit my Grandmother Jennie Ross. When we drove up in their yard, my Granddaddy Fred walked out and said, Did you know we've been attacked?

I did not remember this. My parents told me. They did not know my future husband was out there in that wrath of black smoke and dying men, machine-gun bullets strafing across his deck, cutting down his shipmates right and left.

Pearl Harbor changed his whole life. He never liked guns, hated loud noise, and became deeply offended when people bragged about their war adventures. He never asked for his Pacific service medals. And rarely spoke of his own experiences.

But he told me, deep in those Crusoe nights when the night was thick with leaf and shadow, he told me about the screams and the horror. And he told me again with the heavy smoke hanging over Bladen County.

He had no rancor, no hatred for the Japanese. As he had no animosity for the swamp fires burning to the north. He just had practical plans, the after-effects of attack, the result of hard lessons. The main thing was to stay close together.

We walked outside and stood listening awhile in the front yard, feeling the haze crawl over our sticky skin. Soon, I thought, the wind will shift. We'll have to leave here.

Fortunately, the wind didn't shift and the fires were contained farther north. The Great Dismal survived, and the bottom lands and the floodplains. The smoke drifted off, absorbed, I imagined, in the returning fresh air and the dear old familiar sun that soon brightened and strengthened.

Melissa in the kitchen sink

That water I planned to use to fight fire, full of minerals and iron, was tea-colored, as dark as Singletary itself. It rushed out of the tap looking clear. Then settled and colored. Anything I cooked, laundered, or bathed turned rusty red. Rice. Baby diapers. My very fingernails. I used big green cans of Zud to scrub out the bathtub and sinks, scouring round and round, the sharp smell of the Zud bubbling with the dark water, round and round down the drain. It puckered every finger. Outlined every whorl and curlicue of my fingerprints. My nails looked hennaed.

I had never been around such strong water as this, wild water. My grandmothers knew stronger water, water harder to come by.

Martha Anna Smith cranked her water by a windlass, the water brimming and sparkling in a huge bucket as it hit the light of day ten feet or more up from the dark slate-rock well. Jennie Ross had a tall hand-pump in the backyard. She kept a tin cup and a dipper hanging there. The cup had a little spot of rust. As a child, I thought that rust made the water all the more refreshing. These women would think my water supply, despite its minerals, a luxury.

And the water, other than its stubborn color, was healthy. Clyde collected samples and sent them to the state health office in Raleigh and they always tested clean. I put Melissa in the kitchen sink full of bubbles. Under the bubbles, the water winked dark and fragrant. Melissa didn't care. She slapped the bubbles around, blew them off her hands and knees, gulped the water. The bubbles smelled sweet. And Melissa came out of the bath smelling sweet.

And the coffee, I noted, always tasted good, the soup piquant, and after a while Clyde and I just got used to brown rice, not the natural grain, but with an iron tint. It didn't hurt us. That iron mineral water in our house seemed to match the dark water of Crusoe, to complement it. The lake water, too, left a stain on my bathing suit, darkened my finger and toenails. But that water, too, stopped thirst and washed clean and steeped a long time in my fibers.

4
Strange Threats

MELISSA WAS NOW EIGHTEEN MONTHS old. She and I played a long time on the west side of the house, a fine fragrant spring day, the smoke gone, no fire threats. She ran and pulled long squirrel-tails of gray moss behind her. She built little houses in the sand, and I stuck pine cones on top for chimneys. And as Melissa charged to knock them off, the gray moss festooning around her, a fighter plane from Fort Bragg, about fifty miles to the northeast, suddenly tore across the sky, making that ear-splitting noise, and swooping so low I read the numbers on the fuselage.

My baby screamed and hit the ground, rolling like a little cub until she felt herself well under the lobelia bush that flourished out of that white sand big as a shed. There she stopped rolling and panted like an animal. When I picked her up, her eyes were so widely dilated, they had no color, only big black pupils.

—Oh, God, Melissa! I tried to comfort her. Melissa, it's all right.

But all Melissa knew was something big and loud and swift had come out of a perfectly blue sky. Bad! she kept saying. Bad, bad, bad! Then buried her face in my armpit, snuffling around, it seemed, until she got the true scent of her mother and then she began to cry.

I took her inside, enraged at the pilot who could scare a child. Clyde, trying to comfort me later, pointed out the pilot probably didn't even see us, couldn't have. He was swallowed up in a big fierce rush of noise and power. There was nothing personal in it.

But remembering Melissa's dilated eyes, I felt it was personal. I knew Clyde was right, of course. Still, still, I needed something to blame for this shock. I put Melissa down for a nap and sat by her crib on the floor, patting the mattress, patting the blanket, tugging to reassure Melissa, It's all right.

Aerial bombardment, I remembered I read once, was the worst predicament a person could face. A fighter plane attacking out of a seemingly peaceful sky. Nowhere to hide yourself. And as I held my soft and panting child there in the middle of those Bladen County woods, no tanks, no bullets, I remembered that article, and wondered what told Melissa to fear the loud flying object. It had become a contemporary archetype, the article claimed. Children might be born with it.

I only knew Melissa was so frightened, not even I could calm her. Not even my presence was enough for Melissa. She had to hit the ground and roll until she got under something big and safe and impersonal, a common lobelia bush. The article explained how chicks crouch in natural fear of a hawk's shadow. They'll do it whether a hawk is actually up in the sky or not. You can cast a shadow from a cardboard hawk or a kite, they'll run and hide. The old hen never taught them to do that. They just know.

And so, too, I thought now, might Melissa Miller. I sat by the crib a long time. I got a cramp from sitting on the floor so long. Clyde looked in at me, smiled, shook his head. He went to the kitchen and started dinner. I was glad for that. Good old Clyde.

If anybody had knowledge of aerial bombardment, he certainly did. Although reluctant, he let me write it up, that memory of a real hell, a genuine threat, for Pearl Harbor Day the next winter. I published it in the *Raleigh News and Observer*, along with a picture of him and Melissa on the shore of Singletary Lake. He got letters and postcards and phone calls from other Pearl veterans. From women whose sons or husbands or brothers were lost that day. They were hungry for some little flash of remembrance, just any little thing that could put them closer to the person they'd lost. And it hurt Clyde, I could see, and I was sorry I'd written the article, broken into and pirated his peace that had been built so carefully from stubborn oblivion.

Clyde answered all the inquiries. They wanted to know if he had known their loved one, just a passing acquaintance, maybe, on the beach in front of the old Royal Hawaiian Hotel? A beer in a Waikiki bar? It hurt him to write and say, no, I didn't know your brother. I think maybe your husband was on another duty. Your son's name sounds very familiar, but I can't say for sure.

He had a real island, Oahu, with good times spent on it despite the attack on December 7, 1941. The little kids he saw eating sea urchins in tide pools, their lips purple from the juice. The surfing and spear-fishing at Palooa Point, Wainai, the algarroba trees and cactus and pineapple fields.

Sometimes things just came out of nowhere in Crusoe. Fighter planes, people. And all were ways, I figured, I could get information. More than just going to the mailbox across the road. More than the phone, the television. For when you live in such stunning and beautiful isolation, every event, every manifestation brims with meaning. I grew sensitive to nuance, to tone of voice, subtleties of facial expression. Clyde was always sensitive to those things. The isolation affected him as much as it did me. And his reactions were very practical. He never considered anything mystical, no old women with gingerbread in the woods, no bears to threaten sleeping children, no demons. He kept his park like a prize. His days spun like a top. And such practicality made him powerful, I believed. A power I admired and envied. And a power I often wished would fail, just a little, just enough to let something get out of whack.

Things got out of whack for me. Our first October there, I knew I was pregnant. I sought out a physician in Elizabethtown and got it confirmed. It didn't feel confirmed, though. I suspected it was wrong somehow. I came home and took Melissa on my lap. Melissa was cozy in a little blue coverall, her hair fastened with bright barrettes shaped like blue bow-ribbons.

—Mama, she said, you read this book. And held up a book with a blue cover as bright as her coverall, as shiny as her bow-ribbon barrettes.

I took the book, opened it to the first page where the picture showed a little girl standing in front of a storm cloud.

—A big WOOOO! came out of the woods, I read, feeling Melissa shiver and giggle.

—WOOOOO! echoed Melissa. Then rushed off to find her bean-bag clown she called Woo, a little handful of beans stuffed inside pantaloons of calico with a inked grin and arched brows. Woo! she returned and dumped the clown in my lap. That Woo, she said, *that* Woo.

I said to Clyde that night at dinner, Melissa's still a baby herself. What will we do with another so soon?

Clyde looked at me carefully. He smiled. We'll just live, he said. We'll just live. But somehow the simple truth and power of his reaction did not reassure me enough. I wanted something more. I didn't know what.

The next day it happened. I barely had time to get used to the idea of another baby, when it was taken away from me. I huddled in the middle of our bed, a mound of pain and disappointment, pulling the quilt tight to my chin. I listened to Clyde in the kitchen filling the hot water bottle. Then a patter of steps as Melissa came carrying the clumsy rubber vessel, holding it as if it were an animal, a skinned rabbit or a plucked chicken, grinning, a little trail of water sparkling behind her.

—Here yo' hot waw! she announced, attempting to fling it onto the bed.

As the weather turned, Clyde built lots of bright fires, kept the house cheery, entertained Melissa with books and games, bundled me in blankets and provided plenty of good company. And so I recovered. If Clyde was disappointed, he never said. He only remarked once, You always wonder, you know, what the baby might have looked like, what kind of eyes, hair, what it might've sounded like. What little nuances of expression it might've had.

I knew this was the reassurance I'd been looking for that night at dinner. When Clyde's response had been, We'll just live.

The next year, 1963, brought another baby. This baby was due in late September, a date close to Melissa's birthday. Clyde was amused by that. See, he joked, I always aim true. I always hit the mark. Three years, I bet, to the very day.

Melissa and I got in the habit of taking afternoon rambles throughout the long summer. I thought this new pregnancy sharpened my wit, brought me dimensions of awareness, and made me a powerful woman of the backwoods, so naturally and curiously wily.

That's why it startled me the way those same three black women from across the road slipped up. They appeared in the front yard, standing like three shadows at the end of the walkway between the laurel bushes. Melissa and I were getting ready to take a ramble around the park when I noticed her gazing down that way. And when I looked, there they were, gazing back, mild expressions, patient and quiet.

I wondered how long they'd been standing and watching. I went on down the walkway, leading Melissa. By chance, Clyde came out of the park office and came over at the same time. I felt rescued.

—Good evening, I said to the three women. Can I help you? And this time I learned their names. The old one with the snuff brush was Regina.

—This here Omega, she said, scratching one hip. And that one Elise. She the baby sister.

They wanted Clyde to go hunt up Omega's son, Ivory McCoy, who was fishing somewhere on Singletary Lake.

—His wife just get through having a baby, Regina said, and the baby got to go to the hospital, I think.

Regina squinted against the sun. If you can't find Ivory, Captain, she told Clyde, who had come around in his patrol car, we needs you to take the baby to the hospital in your car.

As they stood there discussing this, Ivory McCoy came driving up in what looked like the old truck we saw on blocks that night of the brush fire. Ivory slowed down, looked annoyed, and demanded of Regina, What you be wanting?

—You sorry excuse fo' a man, she said, Loretta done gone and had the baby and the baby got to go to the hospital. Maybe Loretta, too.

I was puzzled that Omega, whose son Ivory was and whose grandchild they were talking about, didn't say a word, just squinted like Regina and shaded her eyes with her hands.

Ivory relented gruffly, Go on, get in.

The three women piled into his truck, Regina and Omega in the cab. Elise, the youngest, climbed over the bed and settled with a satisfied flump, tucking her skirts around her thighs.

As they drove off, Regina reached a dark hand through the window toward Clyde. Captain, she thanked him. The soft inside of her hand gleamed pink as a shell.

He nodded and they left. Omega still hadn't said a word.

The baby was jumping like crazy inside me. I clutched at my high abdomen and marveled at the coincidence. A healthy baby here, almost ready to be born. Another baby across the road born but needing help.

And those mysterious sisters, Regina, Omega, and Elise. And Ivory McCoy. Loretta. They were fast becoming part of my isolation, part of Singletary Lake Group Camp, the wilderness I'd come to call home, working themselves into my life in ways I felt were important. I wondered what I was doing in a place like this, a place that was theirs. Now I was beginning to see I wanted to tell stories about it. Show the significance of such places and such people.

I had been writing stories and poems all my life, and had studied with Randall Jarrell at the Woman's College in Greensboro. Others in my family wrote and published books, my aunts and uncles, my father. So it only seemed a natural thing I would write books. On every sort of subject. I had stacks of spiral notebooks full of notes and lists, starts for poems, starts for stories. Nothing finished.

Now I promised myself when I got home from the hospital in September, after I put my new baby safely in his wicker carriage, made sure he was fed and soundly sleeping, I would get out my old Royal portable with its faded ribbon and write a story about three silent black women standing at the end of my walk. About Loretta having a baby across Kelly Star Route deep in the same woods where my own baby slept. About Ivory McCoy fishing in Crusoe waters, staying down there on the pier all day until those three mystifying women searched him out.

It would be thrilling. I would get up in the night to feed my new baby, and to spread out my story around him, to sit rocking and remembering until he slept again. I would write this story straight through to the finish.

Those afternoon rambles with Melissa taught me other things as well. Things I was not so certain I could understand. Things wild and curious. And scary. Things to flavor a story and give it presence. Such as the thing Melissa saw in the road.

The park road, asphalted and graveled, bumped in some places, smoothed out in others. Melissa and I always came to the curve of the road and regularly paused there at the park gate. But this time Melissa looked down and saw a figure formed by some spilled, dried-up asphalt.

—A mama! That a mama! she ran to it and stomped on it with both feet, her face turning red in the August heat.

It was as mysterious to me as the three women in the yard a few days before. And, again, I couldn't figure out how easily it had slipped up on me. I clearly saw the figure under my child's feet. Long hard loops of asphalt outlined a female body swelling out front, no head and no feet, but with an obvious big belly that infuriated Melissa. She stomped on it a long time. And when she thought she had destroyed it, that thing she called a mama, Melissa resumed her usual pleasant disposition and we walked on as if nothing had happened.

Does she see me like that? I wondered. A lumpy outline of asphalt in the road. A big belly with no arms and no feet. A head with a big mouth. And what was I supposed to do? It was the first time I'd ever seen Melissa show violence: *stomp, stomp, stomp. A mama! That a mama!*

Where there demons after all in these woods? A shotgun in the hands of an old grandfather?

Other than banging a doll's head against the floor on occasion, this child never hit things, never tore up things. It worried me, and I told Clyde that night in bed, as we lay there watching a white moon blossom across the tops of the trees. The big moon seemed to accent and sharpen my need.

—Oh, Clyde said, it's nothing, she's just probably playing a game. That's all. Just playing. Are you sure she said it was a mama?

The pleasant moonlight slid over his big shoulders, washed the bed, and pooled up in the corners of our room. Yes, yes, I said to his last question. She said it was a mama. Then I pulled closer to Clyde, echoing his words, Probably just a game. Just playing. Like you said.

But in the night I dreamed old Regina squinted at me again. Little boys, she said, you treats mean as you likes. But when it comes to lovin, ain't nothin like a girl. Then she cackled and twisted the wool on her head. You a mama! she taunted. You the baby's sorry excuse fo' a mama.

And the manner of Regina's taunting and the twisting of her hair struck me with dread, inside my dream there in the middle of thousands of acres of forest and sand drenched in white moonlight, dread that Regina was indeed the old witchy woman of my suspicions. And that Regina had done some strange harm to me and to Melissa and to the baby unborn.

But as soon as the dread struck me, I woke. The intensity of the dream evaporating all around me, down to my fingertips which indeed tingled as if they'd been drained of feeling for hours and just now felt blood return. I got out of bed and went to look at

Melissa. The child slept quietly, her skin smooth as a peach, her hair like a cloud.

I stood by Melissa for a long time. I reached to gently wind a curl of Melissa's hair around my finger. *You a mama! You the baby's mama!*

Then the image of Melissa's feet stomping and stomping.

What was this fierce love?

I began to look at the woods, at Crusoe's Island and all its people, with suspicion.

Then there was the matter of the snake one morning as we walked back from the big mailbox out beside Kelly Star Route. Melissa had on a pair of little red Keds without socks, bare legs vulnerable to the world. I browsed along with the letters and magazines. Things got too quiet. I looked back. The baby was standing perfectly still, studying something between her feet.

—What that might be? she asked.

A very small copperhead caught in an S under her Keds. She had stepped on his head with one foot and pinned him down with the other. I said, Be still, Melissa, and eased behind, grabbed her up and ran. The copperhead whipped around, his heart-shaped head pulled back to strike. I watched him glide away over the leaves. He was small, but Clyde had always warned me pit vipers were deadly the minute they were born.

I put Melissa down and watched her run on to the park office to tell her daddy, red Keds spanking the road. What if she'd stepped on the snake's tail first instead of his head? We were twenty-five miles from Elizabethtown and the nearest emergency room.

Well, then I would be like Regina, Omega, and Elise looking for Ivory McCoy: *My baby needs to go to the hospital. My baby got snake bit.*

Clyde sent the park attendant back out there with a hoe to find the copperhead and kill it. But the snake was long gone. And now I knew the woods were indeed beautiful and deadly. As natural as breath itself, and as unpredictable. I would put snakes in my story, and fighter planes from Fort Bragg, and little girls who stomped on things. I would put old black women who gave warnings. I would put Clyde. I would go home right then and remember in my story how he saved Melissa from strangling back in Stanly County, when we still lived outside Morrow Mountain. No snakes. No fighter planes. Just plain wooden crib bars painted white.

We didn't have a crib bumper. We never thought of such things. She was only a few months old. But that Saturday morning I heard the baby shriek with pain and fear, I ran in to find her head wedged between the crib bars, the bars crushing in so hard I couldn't pull her out. I panicked, *Her neck will break! Her skull will fracture!*

I called Clyde in from the kitchen door and something in my voice got him there in a second. He was bare-chested, wearing only Bermuda shorts, the fall weather still warm, and had been mowing. He saw the danger right away and with a strong and determined pull, parted the bars and set her free. I was so glad to have the baby in my arms and soothe her cries, and I thanked and thanked Clyde until I sounded silly thanking him.

The sight of his back and shoulder muscles uniting and straining to part those crib bars and set free a baby's tender head stayed with me and told me things about Clyde. His strength and focus. Things to be told again, written up, shared.

Clyde, Melissa, and the Super Beetle, 1963

But what I actually wrote happened a couple of days later in the most brilliantly sunny morning, under a briskly scrubbed sky blue as a china cup. I positioned Melissa in the bucket seat of the sleek new Super Beetle we had gotten, white and dazzling, a veritable Easter egg of a car. She'd grown out of the old vinyl car seat with its spools of beads. Now she liked to stand beside me and navigate the road. She still, though, had no real sense of how to brace or brake herself, so I got in the habit of holding my right arm out to keep her from going through the windshield at every stop sign.

We chugged down Kelly Star Route toward Elizabethtown. I turned a long wide curve past white sand and turkey oaks already tinged with the first reds of fall. A one-and-a-half story frame house with a rusty shed roof stood in a bare yard. And as I drove past, a little boy in the yard lifted a gun and sighted, took long and careful and deliberate aim at my head and fired.

—He could kill me. I tightened my fist on the wheel. Kill me and get away with it. Did you know that, honey?

I looked over at Melissa, then back at the hostile little boy in my rear mirror. He dropped to the sand, rolled over, and assumed a new firing position, his gun sighted on my shiny wrap-around bumper.

Melissa did not see him. We went by too fast. But she smiled at me, agreed, Uh-huh, uh-huh, Mama.

Tobacco fields spread to the edges of the little boy's yard, almost to the sagging front steps. I amused myself thinking what his name might be as we rounded another long curve and the little shooter melted out of sight.

—What do you think that little boy's name might be? I patted Melissa's arm. Might be, might be, she hummed, what his name might be.

I tried to make it into a game, but the image of the child aiming at me was not a game. I was glad Melissa didn't see him. I kept the Super Beetle dead on fifty-five all the rest of the way, the image of my potential assassin rising and falling like waves against a white empty beach behind me.

Back down the road, our errands loaded into brown paper bags, the fresh smells of celery and apples replacing the stuffy new-car smell, I looked for the little boy. But he was not there in the yard. He had killed all the people he wanted for one day. Still, he had made me feel bad, and suspicious. I hoped I didn't look as mean as I felt, so I gave Melissa's arm another pat.

—There my daddy, she said, pointing as I pulled the car up past the house and shops and killed the engine. I sat frowning as Clyde came across from his office.

He smiled, waved, opened the door to take Melissa. I rubbed my face, surprised to feel it sort of numb. I rubbed harder, trying to rub off the frown.

Inside the house, I plopped my keys on the kitchen counter, put away the groceries, and piled the apples in a bowl. Then put on water for coffee and sat down to think through the shooting again. I was really mad at that little boy. No matter if he was just that, a little boy. I didn't like being fired at, even if it was a big plastic gun from the Ben Franklin Dime store. I wanted to do something to him.

The water bubbled and I poured it over a Chemex filter, breathing the pleasant strong fragrance steaming from the carafe. I arranged the carafe on the table and set out two mugs for me and Clyde, first pouring milk for Melissa and opening her a box of vanilla wafers.

They trooped in and settled around. Clyde helped Melissa get in her chair, then watched me pour the coffee. Melissa dunked vanilla wafers in her milk and sucked them with vigor.

I watched a minute. Wish I could get that much happiness out of something so ordinary and bland.

—You do, Clyde said, you get it out of me. He wiped Melissa's face with a paper towel. Her slurping continued without much interruption.

—Guess what.

—What?

—Somebody tried to kill me this morning on the way to town. Somebody tried to shoot both me and Melissa in the car.

—Who? Who tried to shoot you?

I studied Clyde, then clicked my tongue. You don't believe me, do you, Clyde.

—Well, who was it?

—I don't know. Some little kid playing in the yard.

Now Clyde studied me. He tossed the paper towel into the kitchen trash, smiled.

—Why would some little kid playing in the yard try to shoot you on the way to town, way out here, in the middle of Bladen County?

He stood up, drained his coffee. Tell me?

So I got out the old Royal when he went back to the office, found some paper and rolled it in, and started to tell him.

5
Stories

THAT SUMMER OF 1963, WAITING for a new baby, I began to write more stories, sitting in my favorite place, on the cool hardwood floor beside Melissa's bed while she napped. I held a notebook on my crowded belly and wrote with a blue Bic. After Melissa woke up and had a splash-bath in the tea-dark water, I typed my story on the old college-battered Royal, which I had set up on top of the dryer. It was easier for me to work there. I was too uncomfortable in a chair and my belly pushed against a desk. The dryer was the right height. And I felt better standing.

Clyde came through. Is that a best-seller?

He smiled as I pounded away, the lid to the dryer squeaking as the drum thudded and turned. I liked hearing the dryer work, smelling the clean clothes. No matter that they all had a faint henna color, a mineral pungency. It comforted me to hear domestic machines, washers, dryers, refrigerators. And I liked adding my working noises to theirs.

I didn't answer Clyde right away. He teased and coaxed, but I took myself seriously right then. I had to make it work out.

—What's it about?

I almost hated him for a minute, felt he was an invader. Then, It's about us, I said.

He put an arm around me, rubbed the back of my neck. Who'd want to read about us? The dryer knocked off. I typed to the end of a paragraph. Pulled the page out and stuck it in the box with the growing pile. Then I bent to unload the dryer.

—I don't know. I buried my face in the clean hot sheets and towels. Probably nobody.

Then I obsessed. It seemed the story and the baby were the same phenomenon, growing bigger together, expanding, taking up more and more room. My pile of pages spilled off the dryer and stacked on the floor. Melissa crawled up on the dryer and sat behind the Royal, watching the carriage move, and delighting when the bell rang. I let her pull the pages out. And she was pretty good at it, making only occasional smudges or creases. Melissa's marks made the story more real, I thought, gave it character and voice.

Sometimes when I made notes sitting on the floor, the baby turned and knocked the notebook off my abdomen. I liked that, too, and it comforted me as much as hearing things in my house whir and rumble doing their safe jobs.

I even thought I saw the definite outline of a foot kicking the notebook, then the baby withdrew somewhere deeper inside. I leaned against Melissa's bed and wondered what he'd be like, coming there to those woods, to a daddy who drove around in a black patrol car with a whip antenna, to a mama who typed stories all day on top of the dryer, and to a sister who already knew how to stomp on snakes and outlines of mamas in the asphalt.

Grains of sand cut into the backs of my legs. No matter how much I swept the floors, the Crusoe sand stayed there, cutting into the wax, puckering my skin. I shifted my weight and the baby's, pulling up to look at Melissa sleeping. A line of sweat beaded her upper lip. Nothing so hot as August in Bladen County, the park rangers had told me. I heard a rumble of thunder and, looking out the window, fancied I could actually see the thunder coming across that flat hot land toward us. I would like to run out in it naked, clumsy and pregnant as I was. I would like big clear gouts of rain to run all over me, waterfalls and torrents, whirlpools, hurricanes, floods.

Clyde got a new well dug before September, much deeper than the old one, and struck clear water, free of minerals. It gushed through the pipes still looking like tea for awhile, then cleared up for good. I washed diapers and receiving blankets for our new baby's arrival and they came out pure white, smelling of Ivory Snow. I ran a wet rag over the rows of clothesline strung between two metal T's across the back of the yard. And even though I had a dryer in the house, I hung out dozens of the new diapers. Melissa and I played tag between the long white veils of them, the soft Curity gauze patting our faces and tossing in the sunny wind.

—Di-pas, Mama, she sighed, breathing in the sweet fragrance of clear water and soap, Di-pas.

I made rice, grits, macaroni, anything white, and they boiled up without color. The rust faded off my fingernails. My hands felt softer, and my hair seemed suddenly freed of a wild sediment.

I never got the tea stains entirely scrubbed off the bathtub, that tub I'd filled up for the forest fire. The smell of Zud clung to my skin. And for a long time, I still tasted minerals in my mouth, enough to give an edge to my teeth. The old water stayed with us. Like an old friend, almost, it had stopped our thirst and washed us clean, and its tangy memory was a long time fading.

And I went to bed and dreamed the same minerals, the same taste and dark stain. Except in my dream-story, the minerals turned into terrors lurking just outside the house. Things that clung to me and gave off the smell of rust.

Clyde told Melissa she might get a baby brother for her birthday—indeed, he was expected almost three years to the very day, just as Clyde had bragged—and she told it to the park rangers and attendants. One of them grinned, tightening the new water pipes under our kitchen sink.

—No, he said, you won't get no brother. You'll get a sister. Ain't no boys never born at Singletary Lake. He'd worked there a long time and he knew.

No boys born in these woods, I pondered. Only little girls. And they probably had names like Phiny Rose or Thelma Dale. They slept all night in the dark knotty-pine rooms, clutching teddy bears. Their daddies patrolled the park. Their mamas cooked pinto beans and skillet cornbread. They grew and flourished in the middle of the woods just like sleeping princesses. And they had no brothers.

At least four other families had lived at Singletary, slept and ate and quarreled and loved in the same house. No little boys among them. Then Heather and Clyde Miller broke the spell.

We went to the hospital in late September, and Kirk Miller was born with a full head of dark hair and both eyes open, on a Friday, the 20th, 1963. Almost a perfect three years. Melissa's birthday the next week, the 25th. I thought and thought about it, couldn't believe such good luck, such precision. I gazed at Kirk in the nursery. His dark hair made the other babies look unformed, as if they might still be fetuses.

—That baby lays in here and looks around like he's got the most sense, said Queen Esther Edge, my favorite OB nurse. A lively black woman running over in toothy grins and bright intelligence, Queen Esther had one stiff dark hair under her chin curled tight as a spring.

—Your baby already one hundred years old, she said. He be an old man right now.

When she found out I lived way out in the woods at Singletary Lake Group Camp, a place abundant with varmints and other perils, she rolled her eyes. You out there with all them gators and them snakes. You know what my husband do?

She giggled, straightened the sheets. My husband killed a big old mean snake, long as my arm here, and he put it in the front seat of the car.

Queen Esther held out her arm to demonstrate the size of the snake, then bent it back toward her plump bosom. I come along and open the car door and I scream and I have a fit and he like to kill hisself falling-down laughing.

I laughed too. Queen Esther was very good at this. I made a note to remember, put Queen Esther in my story, a wholesome foil to the three mysterious black sisters across the road.

Queen Esther propped a hand on her hip. I be so mad at my husband putting that snake in there on the front seat of the car, you know what?

I nodded and shivered in my safe bleached-white sheets. Queen Esther declared, Looky here, I be so mad, I wouldn't never go ride in that car again. Not after that snake be in there.

I had to agree with her. Who knows what an old dead snake was capable of? Something might get through, snake evil, snake poison, seeping through the upholstery, infecting the flesh of any woman who sat there.

—Don't you never let your husband do nothing like that, she said and rolled her eyes at Clyde in the door.

—Hey, he grinned, you know that snake didn't do a thing in that car seat. Couldn't harm you.

Queen Esther ignored Clyde, bent over me. Don't pay no attention to what he say, honey. Now, I go get that baby. He be hungry.

To take him home, we wrapped Kirk up in fresh new blankets, blankets sweet and clean from that new well water out at Singletary, and Queen Esther Edge carried him down the hall behind us. Slow down, she said, ain't no need to go so fast.

She sauntered along, taking as much time as she could just carrying a little bitty baby. You ain't supposed to go tearing out of here right after you just had one of these things.

Out at the car, she handed the baby over, making little adjustments to his blanket. You take this baby home and raise him big as his old daddy, she said. Next time I see this here baby, he better be big and mean. You hear me?

She flashed a generous smile, and I wanted to tell her how beautiful she was, how funny and wise. I wanted to pluck out the dark stiff hair under Queen Esther's chin and wear it for a charm.

Instead, I just promised her all the things she'd asked, that I would raise the baby big, mean, capable, funny, wise.

—You better. I hear tell you ain't raising this here baby like I done said, I'm gone come out in them woods and raise him myself. It seemed a special blessing on Kirk, on us all, to have Queen Esther Edge say those things over him. *I'm gone come out in them woods!*

We drove down Kelly Star Route back to Singletary Lake Group Camp, all the trees looming into view, crowding each side of the road, the dark lake sparkling to the left, and I told

Melissa peeking round the door, Superintendent's House, 1963

Clyde that for the first time, now Kirk was born and among us, now for the first time in three years, I felt like I was really going home.

—That makes me feel good, he said. That makes everything all right.

We drove through the park gate and up to the house in the sandy yard. Inside we settled our new son in his wicker carriage, an old brown basket on wheels, red wheels, actually painted in memory of that '37 Plymouth which had passed from this life back in the winter. Now we drove the trim white Super Beetle. Our life was moving upward, new car, new baby.

Clyde picked up the baby. Hey, little boy, he said, you're a pretty little boy. Did you know that? Did anybody ever tell you that?

He hugged Kirk awhile, then, You take him, honey, he said, he doesn't like to smell my breath.

—Clyde, I said, a little baby doesn't care what your breath smells like.

Melissa wasn't jealous. She liked having the baby around, except when he cried, and then she cried, too. Stick it in his mouth, she told me, make him stop.

And so I would sit down and nurse Kirk while Melissa stood at an elbow and watched, her own tears snuffling away. I could tell she approved. You stick it in his mouth, she said, as if she thought I might forget.

The family came to view the new baby. Aren't you glad you had a boy? my mother asked. Now you don't have to have any more. She made it sound as if the effort might have been wasted had I birthed another girl.

—I hope he lives up to his good heritage, said Clyde's mother. He comes from good people.

My Grandmother Martha Anna Smith birthed three girls before she had a boy. My Grandmother Jennie Ross birthed three boys before she had a girl. They didn't make differences among the sexes or talk about what kind of good stuff they came from. Children were children. They made little white woolen caps for them in the winter, little cotton sun bonnets for them in the summer. It didn't matter. You got the children safely here, alive, and went with things. Grandmother Jennie told me when Melissa was born, I didn't raise my babies. I just let them grow.

But here these younger and more modern grandmothers were fashioning Kirk's life for him ahead of time. He had to be one thing or another, doctor, lawyer, but most of all, a boy. Then both the grandmothers startled me with, You should move into Elizabethtown now. Now you've got two children. They could go to Sunday School, have little friends to play with. It'd be much better than staying out here in these woods.

They wanted Clyde to live there in the woods by himself all day, then drive to Elizabethtown for the night with me and the children. They wanted me to be a regular mother with neighbors at the fence, Girl Scouts selling cookies at the door. They didn't take Singletary Lake Group Camp, much less my secret Crusoe's Island (which they didn't even know about), seriously. They were chipping away at the oddity, trying to tame Heather and Clyde, make us normal.

—We always said, they added, you should live in town and let Clyde drive back and forth. That's the way it usually is with people. You think?

I couldn't yell at them. They were our mothers. They stayed a while longer admiring the new baby, playing with Melissa, then they drove away, the long three hours back to Stanly County, red clay, rolling hills, flint rocks, the Yadkin River valleys.

It surprised me that somebody could criticize the way we lived, could find it lacking. Just because it was in the woods or beside an isolated lake fifty miles round trip from Elizabethtown. They didn't understand it as I was beginning to feel I did. Though I now felt at home in it, a warmth and a familiarity brought about by Kirk's birth, I still recognized the perils, the possible demons. There could be bears, there could be old women with gingerbread houses, there could be a little shooter standing in the yard. But right now, for me, cocooned in the fragrant perils of Crusoe, there was a new baby to take care of, a little girl to nurture, and stories to write down.

I spread my pages out again. The story had two family murders, a particularly ugly suicide, and rampant madness. The characters came from a good southern family, pleasant and civilized, yet they did bad things. It began to make me anxious about my own two children. I didn't mean to write an evil story, just a very tense and scary one. I wanted to make people take to their beds. And pay attention.

—Who do you think is really going to read that? Clyde asked again. He stirred his coffee and studied me.

—Nobody, I said. But I wrote on and on as the weeks passed into full autumn and all the turkey oaks lost their bright red leaves. My favorite season. Piles of leaves covered the sand now just as drifts of yellow oak pollen covered it in the spring. The air had an exotic touch, fragrant and teeming with something. I wondered if people had their beginnings in an ancient oak pollen that floated down from space. And then it warmed up once it hit Crusoe sand, or floated out across the dark lake. Like the rings of Saturn, maybe those rings of pollen, or masses of red leaves, floated across the flat cola gloss of Singletary Lake. And then made something. A man, a woman, two little children in a house.

I told Clyde what I'd just thought. He said maybe it was just a big compost heap we all crawled out of down here. Pollen and leaves and the rings of Saturn were good for poems, he said, but the fact that we could even think of such things was more significant, say, than the planet Saturn, which couldn't think of itself. Ever. He sort of made me angry, but I knew it was true. And I loved him for saying the truth.

But I unrolled another truth through my story:

Our house, I wrote, did not sit in the smack middle of the four thousand acres of dark woods, but to the southwestern edge. A modest house. A house that did not invite terrors. But the terrors came anyhow. All kinds, big kinds, little kinds. All I had to do was wait.

And I didn't worry in my story except late in the afternoon when long blue shadows shoved through the pines and billowed with a pungency I liked but did not entirely trust. The sun blazed a moment. I watched tiny dusty insects glisten through its red bars. Then it sank.

And I worried then about a bad man getting in the house. I went to each one of its three doors, unlocked and relocked each one. The front door with three diagonals of heavy glass set up high, higher than Melissa's reach. I had stuck swirls of imitation stained glass in the middle of the largest diagonal, bright green and yellow, little prizes we got out of Melissa's Crackerjacks.

It cheered me to have the green and yellow swirls blurring what was otherwise a sharply defined plan: three diagonals set without much flourish, some designer's vision of style ending up on a Sears and Roebuck door attached to a North Carolina state park house.

Then at the back door in this story, I stood longer, gazing at the white sandy yard tufted in Carolina ipecac and dark geoasters. They come apart in your hand, I blinked, my hand exploring the lock. They explode and smudge. This door had a standard three-over-three window set in the top half. Anything, anybody, could come up on the step and look in. No porch. No entry. Just the bald door opening to the bald yard.

In my story, as in real life, we had turned this back part of the house into a nursery, setting up the wooden crib, the bathinette, and the little white chest of drawers. Across its long bank of windows, I put simple curtains, clean cotton sprigged with tiny nosegays. And into my story I put my baby, the boy we planned for, Melissa's brother. And it worried me, I saw, getting up in the night, passing the windows. The sprigs and nosegays couldn't hold back the bad man.

I went to the hungry boy in the crib anyhow and picked him up and held him close, liking the warm little muscular feel of him, his eagerness, his quick satisfied feeding and melting back to sleep. The story was a good one, one I held on to and groomed and trained. I rocked the story through the typewriter as I rocked the baby. And when I put the baby back in the crib, I pulled the curtains closer.

The third door was in Melissa's room, a room that had once been the park office. Nobody in my story, nor in real life, used the door. But it had an impressive rise of brick steps outside, a brass-mounted light, and a big handle with a lock. I had hung curtains over the door and pushed a bed against it. Sometimes Melissa stood on the bed, her head under the curtain, trying to look out the high square pane of glass at the top of the door.

I began to dread this door especially. Opening right into my little girl's room. Right outside my own room. The bad man, if he wanted, could climb the brick steps, stand there and look in at Melissa while she slept. Or at me and Clyde. Clyde, I wrote, would be snoring and unmolested. But I would struggle awake and stare back, a slow fear flashing over me, prickling up the hair on my head.

Then he would sneak around back and look in at the baby, maybe tapping on the windows, making the baby roll over and look at him. I envisioned my friendly baby raised up on his arms, dark head bobbing, grinning back at the man who stood and stared and stared.

And all the time in the story I wrote, the woods got closer. And all the time I could see how they got closer. From one square and unadorned window in the bathroom, I watched those pine woods loom in a thick fringe at the edge of the sand, the sand tufted with sour ipecac. The woods kept creeping up. And I saw it any time I wanted, in the hot blaze of the autumn day. Or at night, when I got up to feed the baby, to check Melissa, then sat on the cold white toilet lid and just watched out the window across the sand at the pines.

Getting back in bed with Clyde, though, always soothed me. And then for a long time in the night, I didn't care how closely the woods crept up. Nothing but woods out there. Clyde took it all away, shoved it over with his deep and steady breathing, a big arm showing on top of the cover. I liked the way he looked turned on his side. I slipped my hand over the muscles in his arm, relishing the strength, basking in the clear and solid reality of the man.

—Where've you been? He stirred, shifted his weight and reached a hand to me. You went somewhere?

I nudged closer, then said, I was looking at the woods. The woods are creeping up.

Clyde listened. I guess they look ominous, yes. But, just woods. Just the middle of Bladen County. Not creeping up.

Then he added, as he always did, his remedies. I can get us a dog. I can get Four County Electric to put up a big light at the shop.

He took me in his arms. Nothing's creeping up.

And we lay there in my story, talking quietly and listening to the night sounds, the chirping of creatures in the woods, the breathing of the pines. And I listened to Clyde, to the night moving beyond the doors and windows, and to the occasional stirrings of the children. Then I drifted toward sleep with these good things for anchors.

At morning, though, I rose on an elbow, my head nodding like the baby's, and blinked. Out in the strengthening sunlight, the same woods looked at me with long and powerful patience. Clyde dressed, pinned the badge to his gray uniform shirt with its embroidered dogwood patch. *Dogwood, the Carolina state tree. Or is it the state flower?* I started to ask him, but the phone rang and he was off into the steady business of his day.

And somewhere in the business of my day, in the curious business of this story I wrote, the late afternoon approached again. And again I waited for Clyde to come back and fill the house with his comforting smell of pine needles and sweat, his strong health, the deep and encouraging resonance of his voice just saying, Hey, what're you doing?

I had to stay on guard. The bad man could get in. If not the bad man, then the woods. I had to be ready at a minute to grab my two children, Melissa in hand, Kirk under arm, and pull down the swing-away attic stairs, hurry up, pull the stairs back, and then huddle, keeping Melissa and the baby quiet—*Oh, God, how to keep them quiet!* All the time listening to the terrors prowling the house below us.

I might drop the baby between the rafters. No floor in the attic, just a few pieces of plywood put down to walk on. I could see his dark head disappear in the thick insulation. He would smother. Melissa would fall, cry. How was I going to keep my children quiet and save their two lives?

I gritted my teeth in the story. Something I did at night, fast asleep. It ran in my family. Night-grinding the dentist called it. I hated him telling me that, with the taste of steel and clove filling my mouth, the weight of the lead apron on my front while he and the assistant disappeared to make X-rays. I hated the sound of that, night-grinding. I liked grit.

And so I came out of the story, blinked at the pages, shocked to find I was actually gritting my teeth over them.

Melissa and Kirk with their mother's first book, 1964

After Christmas, I finished my story. Kirk nestled in the wicker carriage and watched me. I'd propped the Royal on an old hinged-top pine desk, a family antique, something Clyde's family had given us. As I typed, the machine sneaked down the slant of the desk. After about six pages, the space bar touched the bottom. Kirk watched this procedure peacefully. He blinked his eyes each time I hit the return and the Royal zinged back.

Kirk's dark hair hung in long tufts down to his eyes. When I took him to Elizabethtown, somebody in the Red & White grocery always said he looked like one of the Beatles. He wore little denim overalls with snapper fasteners. He waved his fists at me and smiled.

Why, I asked, did I write such a violent story with that new baby beside me watching? The people in the story killed each other. Things swooped down on them. Things carried them off. Woods kept creeping up on them. Little boys came out in the yard with guns.

In January, I finished the book and sent it off to New York. In February, Hiram Haydn bought it for Atheneum. I called it *The Edge of the Woods*. *Time* magazine sent a photographer from Wilmington. The reviewer captioned the photograph and his remarks with "this new novel is a forest of fears." Readers got the message. Everybody seemed happy for me. But nobody more than Clyde.

—Well, he said, I guess somebody's going to read it now.

Well, I fancied up a curious image, well, I wonder if Omega and Elise and Regina will read it. I wonder if Ivory McCoy. If Queen Esther Edge.

6
Dark House

OUR CHILDREN GREW AND flourished rapidly. It seemed to me that Kirk was an infant one day, then up toddling after his sister the next. The children talked together in a special language, encouraging and instructing each other. And as they grew, they divided the territory into surprising features, made curious maps, gave names to landmarks all their own.

—This place, said Melissa, jabbing a stick into the sand across the road from our house, this is Silk Afternoon.

—Why? I wondered where Melissa got the notion of silk. It was a fabric foreign to Melissa's experience for sure. Nothing but cotton, wool, some synthetic blends, some fake funny fur trim on a cap or a collar. That's all she knew. Why silk, I asked again.

—Because when the sun goes down over there, Melissa shielded her eyes with a hand, pointed with the other. It gets all golden and nice in this part. It gets silk.

She had never touched a remnant of silk in her life, yet Melissa knew, just by hearing the word and by looking at the setting sun, how silk was.

Maybe it was the effect of living so isolated in the woods. Maybe they had a corner on perceptions, certainly on exotic experiences.

—And that one way down there, Melissa added. That one is called Bad Dream.

—Bad dreams come from there? I asked. Kirk came up beside her. He jabbed at the sand, too, with a stick. Bad dweem, he mimicked. Bad dweem.

I waited for Melissa to explain the bad dream place. But she remained gazing down the road at it, a far green swath of pond bay and berry bushes. Finally, she said, It's just Bad Dream.

I decided to take her at her word.

Sitting in the porch swing with Kirk the next summer, I thought the sky looked particularly blue and the turkey oaks a sharper green. A sweet smell drifting from the blueberry bogs made me feel I could sit there forever. Maybe swoon with my face in a child's soft dark hair. It was a moment of just swinging on the front porch, a moment open, so unguarded.

Melissa announced from the yard where she'd been digging, A pig! Coming down the road, a little pig!

I pushed open the screen door and a little pig trotted up to our walk. A plain-looking and amazingly clean little pig, trailing what might be an umbilicus. He delighted Melissa, who ran around calling to him. The little pig bleated and stood perfectly still watching her. She had on a bright yellow sundress and I thought he might be dazzled by her colorful skirt flying around, by her equally colorful shovel and pail. She kept smacking her leg with the shovel, saying, Can we keep this little pig!

Clyde put the pig in the shed with the Dutch door, and then we leaned over—Clyde holding Kirk up—to watch him run around, inspecting all four corners before he settled in the middle of the cool sandy floor.

—He looks like he's got little high heels, said Melissa. She liked his hooves and how he appeared to be balancing on them.

Clyde spread the word and before long, Ivory McCoy came to claim the little pig. He had a car full of children and an impressive woman in the front who had to be Loretta. She was gaunt and freckled, her hair in dreadlocks, each tight braid finished off with a different colored button.

I couldn't help staring at Loretta. Where'd she learn hair like that? Off the television? The children's hair showed no such careful attention. Their hair had been brushed out like Brillo, boys and girls alike, their eyes big and friendly.

I didn't see a baby anywhere for a moment. Then he bobbed up between Loretta and Ivory, his hair brushed out like the others, his little body as perfect as Kirk's. They had to be about the same size and age. He grabbed at the gear shift and Loretta made no effort to stop him. She stared back at me until I felt I'd been measured with the finest and most severe instrument.

—I come for that pig, Ivory told Clyde. He went on to explain how the old sow rejected this one because he was born with tusks inside his mouth. So, every time he go to nurse, she knock him winded.

Ivory laughed, I don't see how he done get across the road and over here, Captain.

He opened the trunk of the car and lifted out two big watermelons and a bucket full of catfish. This for you, Captain. Ivory put them on the picnic table. For keeping that pig.

Clyde thumped the melons, nodded, Thanks.

Ivory grabbed up the little pig and stuffed it in the back with his children. They squealed as vigorously as the animal and laughed. Ivory drove off, and Loretta, like the silent Omega I had met over a year ago, didn't say a word. She never blinked, just sat there in the front like some kind of freckled bronze goddess. A silent woman of the Crusoe backwoods, impressive and regal.

Clyde had to kill the catfish with a hammer and then skin them with pliers, Melissa and Kirk watching everything he did. They weren't a bit squeamish, and the whole thing kindled their excitement and energy. But I hated the sight of the fishes' horns and slimy green skins. After Clyde dressed the catfish, I fried them up golden and crisp in cornmeal batter for our supper. The catfish tasted better than they looked, a delicate flavor, enhanced by coleslaw and hush puppies and icy beer.

The watermelons gave a delicious split! under Clyde's butcher knife, and we ate them on the picnic table, spitting black seeds in the sand, salting each bright red dripping wedge. The children ate until their whole fronts were wet, tee shirts and shorts. Then they rolled in the sand and Clyde had to hose them off before they could come back in the house to get ready for bed.

After bathing and dressing the children in pajamas, I sat in the porch swing again. The woods turned black, thousands of little stars peppered the sky. Kirk curled again in my lap, Melissa nodding at my side, we rocked gently for a long time.

Clyde opened more beer and settled in a porch rocker. After a while he said, That was funny today, with Ivory McCoy's pig. If you wrote that in a story, nobody would believe you.

He didn't mean the pig episode was funny like a joke. He meant something else, peculiar and powerful, like ancient bartering. What went on between him and Ivory had gone on for centuries in such strange isolation as ours: sizing up your neighbor, agreeing to exchange a pig, two watermelons, and a bucket of catfish. Agreeing to live in peace.

I smiled, wondering how I would look in dreadlocks, if I'd be as impressive as the silent and proud Loretta. The children were falling asleep. The fragrance of talcum and shampoo lifting pleasantly from their bodies. Clyde gathered up Melissa, I took Kirk, and we tucked them away for the night. Then fell in bed ourselves, happy and pleased and faintly awed.

Stark energy abided in those bald cypress swamps around Singletary Lake Group Camp, in the tangling odiferous junipers and pines. And the energy left a crushed, green smell as relentless as turpentine or a strange wild urine. Boundaries seemed marked by powerful animals, not the familiar deer, bobcat, or black bear, but something alien.

I felt this alone with the children one late October while Clyde attended a park superintendents' meeting in another part of the state. He was away for two nights, and had asked one of the park rangers to check on us before patrolling the park and securing the gate at sundown. The man did this, knocking at the door, tipping his hat, inquiring did I need anything.

—No, I said. Then the ranger drove back to Elizabethtown, leaving me and my two children surrounded by nothing but thick woods, a big wild lake, and teeming swamp.

I had no weapons, no gun. There was a machete in Clyde's closet, and a big mean ax stuck in the chopping block outside. Clyde's woodpile rose neatly to the east side of the house. He'd gotten us ready for cold weather, cutting and stacking kindling and cedar posts and slabs of good dry hardwood. Nobody in his family would freeze.

I watched the red tail-lights of the ranger's truck wink away, heard the last roar of his engine fade down Kelly Star Route. And there I was, undefended, and with two little children. They weren't afraid. They had me, a big grown-up person, their mother, an authority of the household. So they expressed no anxieties as the sun went straight down and it got dark as Egypt outside.

I made supper, poured chocolate milk, warmed vegetable soup, opened crackers. The children ate heartily, then snuggled around me to hear stories before bed. All these were common, safe, normal things. But I kept glancing at the dark woods outside, kept listening for a prowling beast, for claws, hooves. I thought a person might be there, some enemy watching from the woods. I thought in terms of the wild and the alien.

And after the children were in bed, I settled with the latest issue of *North Carolina Folklore* magazine, a publication I had often sent things to, poems, short articles on Bladen County. A terrifying story, "The Spirit of the Pocosin," only sharpened my jitters throughout the night. And how I loved it, the mysterious death and disappearance of an English surveyor who attempted to penetrate the Dark House Pocosin in the West Dismal Swamp between Washington, North Carolina, and Jamesville. He intended to take a party of men through the Dark House until they came to Diamond City, a sawmill town, then push on to the other side of the Dismal.

People warned him against this, warned the Spirit of the Pocosin would kill him as it had killed others. But the Englishman dismissed such backwoods superstitions and proceeded with his surveying party. When the trail through the swamp got too dark, even at noon, his men refused to go further. He went alone, scorning and cursing them. They waited. They heard a scream, My God! And after a hard struggle through a rather short distance of very dense wilderness, they found his body, scratched, bruised, broken, strangled. They fled. And when they returned the next morning with reinforcements, the body was gone.

The tale thrilled me as I sat in my little house and read it over again and scared myself even more. Especially as the house finished off in those whorled and grooved pine panels was naturally dark, a genuinely dark house. Like the Dark House Pocosin. Clyde often complained how dark the inside of the place was. But when the Raleigh park office considered getting all of the panels covered over in sheetrock and painted pastel, I balked. The natural wood was better, after all, and suited our life, our taste.

We ended up with the outside walls sheetrocked. Those on the inside remained dark and whorled. This will work, Clyde said, the outside walls are the ones that need to be insulated. This will work. We painted the sheetrock a soft sandy color. It set off the panels, made them glow, I thought.

Now I glanced at those dark crowding trees in the yard, their tangled understory. I slipped a hand to my throat, squeezed. I relished such silliness, got almost drunk on it. Then looked up the word pocosin in the dictionary. Coming from the Delaware pakwesen, pocosin meant anything shallow and swampy and peculiar to the southeastern United States. The Dark House Pocosin, according to both folklore and modern experience, was particularly thick and black, a swampy hell with the smell of stagnant water and moss, the smell of panic, a peculiarly pungent smell, elusive and alluring.

I knew that smell, perfumy and irresistible, the smell of a gigantic wilderness like Crusoe's Island. If a person were susceptible enough, it could cast a spell on her, pull her right out of the house even in the night, make her leave two sleeping children behind and go running off in pursuit of crazy things. Despite warnings. Despite good sense. She'd follow that old-time Englishman into the Dark House.

And next I was asleep, snoring on the studio bed in the paneled living-room, except the dream took me right out of that safe warm place and into the Dark House Pocosin. My children had followed me right out, too, in this dream, and stood holding hands next to the picnic table. And they watched big-eyed while an invisible beast brought me to the ground, then strangled and tore me apart.

The dream switched to a coroner's inquest in the Bladen County Courthouse where the two children testified, still holding hands, how they saw the weeds bend, the bushes shake, and something tear up their mama.

On the courthouse steps, sunshine flashing off the polished brass handrailings, Clyde berated the park ranger, How could you go off and leave like that? Didn't you know something was going to get her!

Back at the inquest, the children said they couldn't see what it was. Sometimes they saw Mama, and then sometimes parts of her were blocked from their view. They didn't know such words, such vocabulary as that. But they knew there was something out in the woods they couldn't see. And that it got Mama.

Just as I was starting to feel really sorry for myself, carried off by a vicious invisible beast right in front of my two little children, the phone jangled me awake. Morning light flooded the room. The receiver felt surprisingly warm as Clyde said he'd be back by noon. I got the coffee perking. The children tumbled out from their room to switch on Yogi Bear cartoons. I chided myself, blinking over the first strong cup, for expecting a beast to drag me out of this pine-paneled Whirlpool kitchen.

Nevertheless, one place in the park continued to haunt me exactly like the Dark House. This was a long tunnel of thick swamp trees, green in summer and gray in winter, leading out to the lake. When

I left the bright white sand at the entrance to this tunnel, I plunged into another dimension, smelling bent twigs of juniper, cypress, pine. And especially smelling the pond bay, something as pungent as old-fashioned shaving lotion, that awful bay rum concoction. I used to choke on bay rum wafting from the slick hair of my great-uncles and other old harmless family men who patted me or held me on their scratchy woolly knees when I was a little girl. Just too sweet and overwhelming.

Even in the winter, the tunnel gave off a bruised green smell. And when I came out at the other end, Singletary Lake flashed and rippled like a thousand wet mirrors. I loved the lake, but I hated going through the tunnel to get to it. No other access, except the little canal at the spillway. Or through the swamps.

In the summer, the tunnel was full of mosquitoes. A few mosquitoes still hung around when it got cold, but the tunnel was silent then, and prone to sudden spooky echoes. I was always glad to get to the other end and step out on the long silvery cypress pier, shielding my eyes against the sudden flash of the sun across the water.

Of course, I couldn't just walk through that place like a normal person. I had to make up horror stories and nightmares about dark silent invisible things, the spirits of the pocosin, the alluring and deadly entanglements of a big wilderness. I made up far worse things than the story about the Dark House. I made up dozens of young men, princes, rotting in the swamp, their fingers clutching Carolina bamboo briars. I made up one enchanted woman, a princess, sleeping right in the smack dab middle of the pocosin for a hundred years. And I made up an invisible beast who lurked in the tunnel, a growl starting far back in his throat, a growl that grew and thickened and came out of all sides of the tunnel until the beast brought you to your knees.

Nobody else dreaded the tunnel the way I did. Melissa and Kirk waited a moment at either end, in the bright sand or beside the flashing lake, then shrieked and dashed to stand breathless and red-cheeked waiting for me to dare myself through.

I wouldn't look too far off either side of the path, just glanced occasionally at the cypress knobs pushing through the spongy ground, just barely noticed fiddle-neck ferns, deer tracks, the long murderous coils of bamboo briar. I longed to see the comforting litter of park users, a Milky Way wrapper, a Dixie cup, a Coke bottle.

But Clyde Miller had that path groomed and picked over daily by park attendants. No scrap of paper survived. He scoffed at things lurking in the pocosin. He understood how to make clean getaways. He kept enough gas in the car and put a dead-bolt on the front door. He read books and lifted weights and kept up with the news and weather. His allure was the comfortable bittersweet tobacco, strong coffee, and good honest sweat.

—Nothing's going to get you but yourself, he said. And he meant the woods were the woods, they had no mind, no motive. He had great respect for wilderness and the workings of nature. And he wanted people to relax inside that, take strength from it.

I always pulled my knees up in a fetal curl when I went to sleep. Had done it for years and years, a hard habit to break. But Clyde pulled my legs out straight and smoothed them with his hands.

—Sleep with your legs straight, he said, the feel of his hands a steady, quiet pressure through my cotton nightgown.

—I can't help it.

—Yes, you can, too, he said. This helps, to sleep this way. Gives you more confidence.

—Shut up, I said, first giggling, then sighing. My eyes drooped, stuck together, and I slept, straight-legged and peaceful. And when I woke the next morning, he would be gone to his duties. My legs still straight.

But he had no time for the mystical.

I really couldn't help it. The pocosin was luxuriant and entangling, a killer. Tight branches reached out over my head and locked together. The cypress swamps percolated a slight gurgle. And if I left a footprint, it would quickly fill.

So it was always a relief to break through that tunnel, hurry toward the wide-open and rippling glossy Singletary Lake, the long pier with its friendly orange floats bobbing on dock ropes, and catch up with my children who waited, healthy and unafraid, their eyes bright with generous welcome.

Every passage was a test of my willpower. I had to resist the temptation to let go, turn off the groomed path, and delve into the pocosin. Once out there, the beast and his wilderness would take me by the throat.

The children might hear me scream, run back to the house. And Clyde would find me in the morning with a bamboo briar, thick as his hard tanned arm, wrapped around my throat, every little black and green spike cruel with wild victory.

7

Gentle Beasts

WE BEGAN TO ACCUMULATE PETS, two black kittens, Thomas and Tar Baby, of definite Siamese origin. And a dingy patchwork dog, Poochie. When Kirk chose that dog, I thought he was the homeliest pup in the litter, dirty white fuzz, big sorrowful eyes. I asked, Why do you want this one?

Kirk dug his hands into Poochie's fuzz. 'Cause he feels good.

Now the dog had grown up a little and he looked better. The dirty white fuzz turned thick and tawny. The sorrowful eyes took on intelligence, and he initiated some wonderful games. Like running and tossing up big pine cones to catch, then running and tossing again, barking ferociously all the time. This dog would never sleep in the house Clyde had built for him, preferring to submerge himself in dry leaves when it got cold. The children would go out in the mornings, whistle, and a big brown hummock of leaves near the garage would slowly shudder, sneeze, then fall apart to reveal a happy dog.

Poochie liked to accompany us on our park explorations, but the cats did not. More often they remained home to nap in the sun, Thomas on the front steps, Tar Baby, for some reason, in the lower branches of the turkey oaks.

But for exploring, nosing out fresh deer trails, and plain companionship, the tawny-white patched dog was best. And he seemed always to be around during the most impressive encounters.

Down the dead-end sandy park road, a small canal served as a natural spillway from the lake. Pines and oaks arched overhead and occasionally a flying squirrel let go his safe branch and sailed down like a big flat leaf to a lower one. Deer slipped through the laurel and pond bay tangled around the water. The whole atmosphere was one of quiet discovery, a good resting place.

The low dam wedged across one end of the canal and Singletary Lake spilled over it with a brisk rhythm, wearing away the concrete to expose its little brown and white pebbles and make me crave old-fashioned peanut brittle—the very same consistency and look: lumpy, fragile.

A real bridge once connected our canal with the backwoods of Bladen Lakes State Forest. But now only the old pilings remained, softened over in scarlet trumpeter and moss.

We made this a favorite place, what the children called the Secret Place, though it was open to all park users, fishermen and boaters alike. We liked to catch our breath here, inhaling the bright flash of the lake at the farther end of the canal, following the long curve of thick woods, and finally resting by the rush of dark water over the dam and down Colly Creek.

Each time we encountered people at this special spillway, it startled me. I never really got used to the fact that my home and all that surrounded it belonged to the people of North Carolina. That the woods I rambled through, the dark lake I loved, were the people's woods and the people's lake. Even Clyde, my wedded husband, as a state park superintendent, belonged to the people. It was enough sometimes to make me grit my teeth.

Those people of North Carolina locked themselves in and out of the park at night. Knocked on our door in the middle of supper for a key. Or a camping permit. Or a rowboat. And they invaded the children's Secret Place.

This clear day in March, so bitterly cold I felt my face would freeze and fall clattering to the road, I walked by myself to the spillway. I was taking a break from writing. The children were in Elizabethtown schools, Melissa in the second grade, Kirk in kindergarten, and Clyde was busy in the park office.

My skin stung from cold. Tiny leaves wafted down a long column of sunlight between trees. Wild scuppernongs twisted around the highest limbs, and I wondered why scuppernongs picked out the tops of the trees. Nobody would climb up there to get the grapes.

Poochie ran ahead and left me to these reveries. There was a soft hazy uncertain look to the road. So hazy, I noticed a blackberry bush with all its thorns strikingly clear in the air. I came to the spillway where Singletary Lake ran like dark glass and threads of bright water dripped from the pilings. And there I saw more blackberry bushes with fiery drops clinging to thorns.

Four people: a pregnant woman, a man with fishing gear, and two children, an older girl and a younger boy, very near the sizes of my own children. Poochie was in the middle of them, shamelessly wagging his tail and sniffing each new leg and hand. The pregnant woman talked baby talk, Him's a good ole dog, a good ole feller, yup.

The two children gave me a brief intense stare, then got on with their play, throwing sticks in the water and quarreling. The man wanted to fish and asked me if I reckoned anybody would get him because he didn't have no permit.

—My husband, I said.

Kirk, Melissa, and Poochie, 1966

—Who's he?

—The superintendent.

—Wal, the man said, why ain't he down here where people's wantin to fish?

I tried to deal with it. You got a fishing license?

He said, Yeah, but I ain't got it with me right now.—Well, I asked, What kind of bait you use?

—I use shrimp. He looked me up and down. He knew I wasn't anybody important. It was only the man, the superintendent, who could ask him questions like that.

—Well, I calmly stood there, if you use natural bait, I think it's okay.

I felt cold and stubborn as a stone in my tight jeans with frayed bell-bottoms, a shapeless sweatshirt, and a stinging-red, cold face.

My hair flew around full of electricity, too long and too thick for these people's standards. The woman's pale hair curled short against her scalp. The man's hair was shorn like a convict's. The children's hair matched their parents'.

The man prepared his rod and line and found to his immense annoyance that he was out of bait. Ain't we got no shrimp? he snapped at the woman. Why ain't you told me we ain't got no more shrimp?

Then the woman—she looked close to delivery, actually a rather pretty woman, her lips as pink as an empty shell—said, patting Poochie all the time, Use one of Monette's fingers. And she gave a mean little snicker.

Monette was the little girl. She stopped playing with her brother and looked at us, her eyes as round and her forehead as smooth as her mother's, her pale hair curled against her skull. But her lips weren't empty. Monette's lips plumped full of fury and dismay at the casual power of adults. Her lips pinked, then reddened and parted over small hard teeth.

I could see the little spaces between Monette's teeth. As exact as the blackberry thorns spangled with water.

—Whaaat? Monette drawled.

She couldn't believe what she'd heard anymore than I could. *Use one of Monette's fingers.* The look on her face wavered a moment with terrified wonder, then formed positive hatred, because then she did believe it. Believed as I did that her finger, curled like a shrimp, was stuck on a hook and the hook cast whizzing into Singletary's dark water.

My whole being turned as stingingly cold as my face. Still I stood and stared at these people. *Use one of Monette's fingers.* Of course, it was a joke. I knew that. Monette knew it, too. Still, and still.

The pregnant woman blinked at me and almost smiled, as if to offer me the joke. I blinked back, then whistled to the dog, who twisted and groaned in ecstasy at the woman's feet. She didn't have the thick ankles of pregnancy, but rather slender ones, her feet laced in navy blue Keds with white socks. She rubbed a foot on Poochie's belly, around and around. His hind legs vibrated.

A rush of images ran over me: Isaac, Abraham, sacrifice, shrimp, mongrel dog, a little girl's finger. Maybe if I looked hard enough, there might be a field mouse caught in the blackberry bushes? A better offering for those hard people? Bladen County fishermen declared nothing made better bait than a drowning mouse. Anything will strike it, they promised, *anything!*

I stood it as long as I could, then yelled to Poochie. He wriggled around to eye me, then sneezed, got up and followed me back down the road.

I walked straight to the house, never looking back at those four people who had invaded the Secret Place, and I thought I'd never be the same person again. I rolled paper into the Royal and hammered out my fury. I wanted to tell this ugly little story.

It was a joke. I knew that. They didn't mean it. But the woman said it. The child heard it. I felt the dark truth germinating deep in what one said and the other heard. Even though I couldn't translate it, it was a true evil. It scared me and it scared the child. Such a story ought to make people take to their beds.

An old Bladen County man told me there were ghosts out at Singletary Lake, the ghosts of Yankee and Confederate renegades who had been caught and hanged, their bodies then thrown in the water. He said it was the practice to leave the men's hands unbound. They would hold on to the noose as long as they could. Eventually, their arms would tire, their hands give out. When the posse came back, every neck would be stretched. He told me this, eating a banana popsicle, the sweet syrup melting down the backs of his spotted old hands.

I thought of those wretches hanging there, holding on with both hands to the killing rope, maybe looking out over the flat glossy lake, the moon coming up one last time. Eaten by beasts seemed a kinder death to me. Spotted beasts with old sticky spotted paws.

The old man also told me, practically in the very next breath, that the most beautiful women in the state were raised in Bladen County. When my mother sat in a chair and let her hair down, he claimed, it would sweep over and touch the floor.

He was so proud of it and so taken with the image that he sat back speechless for a moment. Then he shook himself, What was I a'telling just now?

Crusoe's Island, beautiful and deadly, and the old man's placement of his beautiful long-haired mother's story next to the lynching of renegades—these phenomena struck me as particularly apt. Even the banana popsicle was apt. A bland sweet nourishing thing, innocent and mindless, in the middle of natural horrors.

This wild place, elliptical and glossy, dark as cola, washed over a narrow white beach, often washing up smooth pieces of wood we liked to collect. Clyde found a gnarled stump smoothed into a cow skull, something you'd expect to see bleaching on the American desert. And I found a solid cypress limb, shaped like a wolf's head. We dragged both pieces back to the house, wolf and cow, and set them in the yard. I tried to grow marigolds, petunias, zinnias around them. Rain fell on them, continuing the softening process. The children sat on them and we made pictures.

But the closest we came to real horror, natural and innocent, was the alligator. Crusoe seemed a proper place for an alligator. Hot as a steam bath in summer, the sticky smell of cypress resin thickening the air, the lake hosted snakes and turtles, gar and red fin. Birds nested in the hollows of the cypresses. And not many people came around to disturb the solitude. An alligator could live there forever unmolested.

We saw him only once. Clyde took us out in one of the park rowboats, attaching a small motor to the back. He navigated the far shore of the lake, and it surprised me to see things there like old remnants of piers and fish traps, cypresses standing farther out in the water than on our park use side. It was like seeing the dark side of the moon. You get used to one way, I thought, then suddenly you see it has another life all its own, something perhaps more powerful and significant than what you'd thought.

The actual island was a small swampy mound slightly off-center in the lake that lapped its shore. Fishermen and hunters long ago had built shanties all over it, deer-blinds and duck-blinds, a few fish traps. There was no pier, no landing place. Nobody went there, except park patrons who rowed or boated out the same way we were doing. Clyde always warned them about snakes, the occasional black bear, the alligator.

This particular day, he was taking his own family to the island and we were all excited. I packed a picnic. I planned the very place we would step ashore and spread the cloth. It would be easy, pleasant.

Then dead ahead, I saw a floating log. Except this log had eyeballs and a blunt snout. Kirk and Melissa, in the bow of the boat, were trailing their hands in the water. They hadn't even noticed. And when the log turned and submerged, I yelled at them to get their hands out.

After we passed over him, the alligator surfaced, turning slightly as if he wanted to get a better look at us. The children exclaimed, That's the alligator! Then kept their hands clenched close in their laps. They'd both brought along balloons and in the excitement, let them slip away. The balloons dipped, then settled to the dark surface, floating primly as ducks.

—That alligator's going to eat up our balloons!

—It's okay, Clyde and I both said, you can get another one.

And so we left the balloons to their fates. I kept waiting for the alligator to submerge and surface directly under us. The boat was flimsy fiberglass, as vulnerable as those balloons. The alligator could knock a hole through it with one slap of his mighty tail. He would eat us up; our bones would crunch and our blood ripple in oily red circles. It would hurt.

But he lost interest in us, glided off to the far shore. How I would have loved to see him walk out of the water, walk around a while in the tangled brush, then slide back in. He was the archetype for all those ferocious alligators and crocodiles I once watched Tarzan wrestle through hours of Saturday movies in the Badin Theatre.

Then I heard him hollering across the lake. A bull alligator sounds just like that, a bull hollering. Hollering for lady alligators. I would have further thrilled to watch them make love, humping along in the cypress knees and the dark shallows, fearing no spirit, smelling their own honest stink.

He was a hermit, I thought, trapped there by the water or the highway—Kelly Star Route ran right along the western perimeter. Maybe alligators didn't like to make long trips overland to find other alligators. Maybe he was a spirit himself, a dark god of the pocosin. He waited there for the bodies of Yankees and Confederates to be thrown to him. He kept an eye open for one of Monette's fingers. He'd heard all the stories about beautiful women with long hair that swept the floor in Bladen County. He'd watched old men with spotted hands eat banana popsicles.

These flavors crept into the stories, built up and took on color. Like gritting my teeth, these things shaped my habits. And the terror I kept suspecting and dreading to come out of the woods, out of the fields and across the sandy yard to get me and every one of the people I loved, the terror turned out to be, on a particular summer morning, not the bad man I'd imagined, but an animal, a big buck deer, a stag with antlers, charging out of the early mist in a rushing herd—entirely doe, except for him. Charging toward me. And right before impaling me on his rack, turned aside and thundered on to the pines and vanished like the mist itself, every particle evaporating, leaving a faint sting on my skin.

I had come out for my customary early trudge, rounding the sandy park road, through the group camp area, the whole place still cool and silent. Tiny white spiderwebs spread across the wet grass. If I touched them, soft and springy, the dew sparkled off each thread.

I loved this early time. No other hikers, no park workers on the road. Not even my own family, still sleeping back in the house—except for Clyde who sat over a hot mug of coffee, a pencil behind one ear, mapping out his day.

Then the turn down toward the lake. Thick swamp woods on one side, mowed fields and hummocks of sand on the other. My dingy tennis shoes smack the sand. My legs warm to the movement and the strain. I notice a spot of dried cereal on my shorts, brush it absently, thinking, *Raisin Bran!*

Then, oh, then, the mist opens like a soft white curtain and the big deer runs straight at me. I can see him so clearly. Smell the dark wild gamy heat of him, a smell like pine straw and crushed bayberry, a smell like fresh manure, a smell, too—and this faintly relieves me—a smell like your own cozy cat in the hot sun. You reach out a hand to stroke your cat, she purrs, flicks her tail.

But it isn't my pet here. And I stop hard, feeling the sand crunch under my shoes. I stand there for what feels like a long time, though it couldn't possibly have been, I realized later. But I stand there and watch it, live it over and over in my mind, noticing every detail. The black nose, black eyes, the delicate pale hairs on his muzzle. And the thudding hooves, sharp as razors. And right before, just the moment before impact, the animal sees me and he banks with the precision of a dancer, feints, turns. And does not run me down, does not strike me.

I stand amazed. The mist floods over me. I remain alive. I remain a woman things happen to. Surely, surely, this is a good thing.

I continued to stand there blinking, listening to the sounds of the morning around me, feeling the passing of the big deer. Then turned and trudged home, not finishing my walk. I had to tell this to Clyde.

He listened in his usual quiet and bemused manner, sipping at his coffee, yellow pencil behind his ear. His eyes deepened, took on a curious blue as I poured out the details of the mist, the big deer. His eyes fastened all over my face as I told this.

—You were lucky, he said. He could've run right over you.

I shivered, remembering the heavy rack the animal carried. Saw myself again impaled, felt my blood spilling, and the piercing tearing agony.

Then Clyde switched on to something else, to where the deer might have been coming from, what might have spooked him. The middle of the summer, plenty of mast and grazing. He concluded the herd was across the highway, Kelly Star Route, probably feeding in somebody's fields.

—They high-tail it back to the park, you know, when it gets good and daylight.

I nodded. The warm fragrance of Clyde's coffee tingled in my nose. I thought again of the deer's muzzle, each individual hair, the quick astonished flash in his dark eyes.

High-tail it. That's what they did, too. Put up high their white flag of a tail and run like mad, springing and leaping, and then gone.

Clyde gathered his papers and refilled his mug. I'm just wondering, he said, why it was so late, this long after sunrise, they were coming back.

—I don't know. *They came back for me.*

Clyde kissed me. You okay?

Just then I realized I was covered in a film of sweat. And when I raised my hands to his shoulders, my hands were trembling.

8
Taking Pictures

A N ENORMOUS BLACK-AND-WHITE king snake lived in a clump of myrtle bushes by the pier. We came upon him numerous times, always startled by his size, a least five quiet feet of snake lying there. After a moment in which he tried to interpret the concussion of our feet, the king snake slithered away. He made a peculiar rustling in the grass, like old people rubbing their dry hands together on a cold morning. Or paper crumpling. Sometimes I thought I saw the tip of another snake's tail flicking from his wry mouth.

Because the king snake preyed on other snakes, like cottonmouths, we didn't want anybody to kill him. We didn't particularly relish keeping close company with him, either, but we appreciated his help in the balance of life around the lake. Always something spooky about happening upon any snake, even one you consider harmless. Just as soon as you see him, you get the uncanny feeling he's already been watching you for a long time.

We took a lot of picnics in the early spring, trying to get as much private enjoyment out of the park as we could before the opening of the season on June 1 each year. For a while, Clyde kept a small picnic table down at the shore of the lake for us. It was easier than rowing over to the island. We would go there with a basket of peanut-butter sandwiches, a hunk of cheese and box of saltines, carrot sticks, apples, boiled eggs, and a big jug of iced tea. Sometimes we just went with big boxes of cereals, Cheerios and Corn Flakes, and ate them by the handsful, so eager were we to get out there.

And so we went one year, feeling good in the turning of the season, the air balmy and fragrant, swinging the basket, and looking forward to a pleasant Saturday morning. The children darted ahead. Then the stink of something rotten struck us all full in the face.

—Look! the children pointed.

Somebody had killed the king snake and coiled him up on the pier with his mouth open. For a joke.

I dropped the basket on the picnic table, waited while Clyde went out on the pier, cautioning the children to slow down, slow down. They were running right out to the carcass, hunkering down to stare.

I crept up a little closer. The snake could come back to life, I shivered. He could turn on the children, on us all. He could blame us for this. Open his eyes and kill us with his very look, his stinking breath. But he was just nothing but a poor old dead king snake, all coiled up with his mouth open. Never hurt a thing. Somebody had thought him hurtful, hateful, deserving of death. So somebody had bashed him, stomped him, desecrated his body, and left him there for Melissa and Kirk to find.

The children got a stick and poked at him carefully. Then Clyde dragged him off into the woods and they all three raked dirt and leaves over him. The snake gave them one last baleful glare.

Then he was gone into the percolating chemistry of the swamp, irritable, maybe, and shy, and now dead.

The children wanted to know who had done that. Clyde said he didn't know, maybe some fishermen who got scared of him, and didn't know he was nothing but a plain old king snake.

I spread the tablecloth and set out the sandwiches and poured tea. The dry crackle of waxed paper made me look around. But I never saw another black-and-white king snake down there.

A cottonmouth began to show himself at the spillway. And the way we happened upon him made us all angry, as well as scared. No crackling paper, no slithering through dry grass—the cottonmouth lurked there in the shadows like death. Or he appeared sunning, draped loose as a rope over the blackberry bushes. Or sometimes draped himself leisurely across the top of the dam when no water spilled over. He seemed to dare us to make the wrong move.

Clyde wanted to kill this snake. But each time he got close enough to hit him with a big stick, the snake opened up that dead-white mouth, and Clyde decided both his stick and his arm were too short. He sent Melissa and Kirk back to the park maintenance shop for a hoe. Clyde and the cottonmouth kept each other at bay until they returned, running and dragging the long hoe behind.

Clyde went at him with the hoe and missed and missed again. I couldn't stand it. The snake coiled himself over and around the hoe, escaping the cutting edge each time, and backing Clyde away with aggressive undulations. I could hear the rasp of his fangs against the steel. Clyde chopped and chopped at him in the vines and the blackberries.

—He's getting away! yelled the children. Daddy, kill him!

Kirk and turkey oaks

Clyde never killed the cottonmouth. He remained at large somewhere near the spillway, and we walked carefully around that place, flinching at every twig, avoiding dark corners. In bad dreams, I saw his wide white mouth opening and his thick coils gathered to strike. His mouth was like two palms placed together and then opened wide apart at the heels of the thumbs. I never saw a mouth so evil, so dead white. It unhinged and spread flat. And then the strike, clumsy, but deadly. The snake banged his fangs against my arm once, twice.

I jerked awake, almost sick. Sweat ran down my neck. Clyde snored pleasantly beside me. The turkey oaks rustled outside.

Poochie roused, gave one low bark. The children, I knew, stayed safe in their beds.

Clyde's generous brother in California sent me a magnificent present, an Exakta with Penta prism and Carl Zeiss lens. I began to photograph Crusoe's surprises, bear grass and pipeworts, Spanish moss and geoasters and sundews, even a Venus fly-trap. All weathers, all moods. I also photographed the children in the middle of this exotica. I wanted human life as well as natural flora. My girl and my boy, also the dog, the two black cats and their various litters.

And when they bloomed that year, I really wanted to get one of the many white water lilies floating along the canal. They were huge and lush with thick yellow centers. I could already see my enlargements framed and hanging on our bathroom wall. Water lilies poignant and powerful as Monet. So I persuaded Clyde to take me out again in the fiberglass rowboat. I held the camera in my lap and peered into the dark water, searching for the best subject.

Clyde steered with a pole, said maybe the mean old cottonmouth would jump up in the middle of those water lilies. He pushed on the pole and the boat slid closer to a freshly blossomed lily, white and radiant against shiny wet leaves, a whole mass of them spread over the canal. I held the camera to my eye and adjusted the focus. I didn't care anymore about any cottonmouth. I'd forgotten the bad dreams.

I fingered the camera, shifting the angle to include Clyde. He was patiently amused by all this. And I loved the moment, Clyde caught there in the boat on the cola-dark water, and I wanted to catch the moment forever in one clear shot. Put us both in sharp perspective, something the children could hold in their hands and say, *That's what Mama and Daddy did one hot day. Went out on the lake in the boat and made pictures of a bunch of water lilies. Look at this. Look at how good this picture is.*

A quick irreverent splash near us broke this vision, and I turned to see Poochie, the ubiquitous dog, churning toward the lily pads. He held his muzzle stiffly and snorted little clear drops of lake water. His white tail flapped like a flag.

—You dog! I yelled, Get out of my picture.

Clyde told me to be quiet and calm down before I upset the boat.

—The dog's going to get in my picture, I insisted.

Clyde didn't care, said again to calm down. Poochie snorted and churned on. Clyde poled the boat up to the dark floating lilies, and I once more adjusted the focus. The petals sharpened and took on brilliance as the Penta prism picked out each one with its fiery speed. Then, right before I shot:

—Look at that! What did I say! Clyde sounded both smug and anxious. But I refused to look at him.

—No, I kept looking through the camera, seeing the gorgeous lily and then beneath it, the thick heart-shaped head of the ugly snake. And kept hearing the dog paddling ever closer.

—Poochie!

The dog ignored my yelling. Kept on target for the lily and the evil thing beneath it. I witnessed it like a fast-forward movie reel: dog snake dog snake white dark snort fang paw strike muzzle.

—Sit down, be quiet, said Clyde. He pushed on the pole and the boat began to swing around. He'll follow us. Be still.

We glided up to another mass of lilies. I waited until I saw Poochie pause, turn, and head for shore. Then I focused on another lily. A long view of one star-shaped flower poised above shiny split leaves. Pale green weeds stuck up through the dark pads and Singletary sparkled.

I shot. The dart of light struck home and burned a prize water lily into the black fertile film. On the shore, Poochie bounded out, water dripping down each white leg and off the end of his tail. He shook himself, then ran on, nose to the ground, scenting a new trail.

Dumb dog. Never even suspected the perils out in the lake, the deadly things wound around the roots of water lilies. When my pictures came back, they showed a slight snaky shadow under the white flower. And the flower dipped under a heavy yellow pollen in its center. And beyond, blurred by distance, but distinct enough for me to see since I already knew it, the first flower I'd prized glowed like a snowball. The ripples in the water were left by the dog. I knew that, too.

It was a significant moment, I felt. I'd been a good witness. So, I claimed, you call me to any inquest you might think about holding to analyze Crusoe's Island. Or Singletary Lake Group Camp. Or whatever you like to call those woods and cola waters. This is a thrilling place. And I have something to say about it all my own.

And I would say it with pictures and stories and animals and people. With suspicions and with bad dreams. And with little kindnesses. Like those I saw all around me. Like Rayvon's. Rayvon Kinlaw, a huge giant of a man, worked as an hourly-paid laborer at Singletary Lake Group Camp. His wife, Lady Selma, as short and delicate as Rayvon was huge, had raised ten children in the sandy pine woods. Raised, too, a plentiful supply of chickens and hogs, turnips and cabbages. I envied the names Bladen women had: Queen Esther Edge. Lady Selma Kinlaw.

Rayvon came to work in bib overalls, his lunch in a paper bag, and he was perfectly content to stand around and watch things.

He did a lot of watching, Rayvon. Clyde set him to work one after-noon digging a long trench for new water pipe not far from our house. I liked to go by on occasion and see what Rayvon was doing, ask him questions. I never deterred him. Rayvon dug and dug, steady as a tortoise, wiping his face on a bright purple ban-danna cloth, then continuing steady, steady. He smiled and spoke to me, but kept his attentions firmly on the job.

Then one afternoon I found Rayvon stopped, bent over in the trench. And as I watched, he lifted up a little brown toad on his shovel. He set it on higher ground and gently, gently, got it to hop away. Rayvon stood a moment watching the toad. Then he said to me, I bet he thought he was in a *turrrrable* place.

Then on again to the steady digging.

Other big men, big as Rayvon Kinlaw, might have smacked the toad with their shovels. Or stomped it under their feet. I liked that in Rayvon. I liked that very much.

He'd even changed Kirk's diaper once, back when he first joined the park work detail. Clyde, hearing the phone ring over in the office, had left Kirk, a toddler, in the shop with Rayvon. Hot summer, Kirk wore only a big white Curity diaper and a little pair of Keds. When Clyde got back to the shop, Kirk staggered around happily in a fresh diaper, the wet one piled in a corner on a paper towel.

—You change him? he asked Rayvon who was whittling a long piece of yellow pine.

Rayvon spit, wiped his mouth, closed up his knife. Changed a many'em, he said. A many'em.

—It just seems impossible, Clyde told me later, big Rayvon, a natural giant in overalls, would have such an easy touch with a baby.

—Well, I agreed, but he did have ten.

Those bulky white diapers plus Clyde saved Kirk's life, too, that same summer. I had gone to a weekend conference about books and writing, all by myself, Clyde agreeing to take care of both children. And he had taken them to check the lake water level. Melissa strutted out to the end of the pier, she was a confident four years old, and she could handle herself in such a place.

Kirk, nowhere as steady, toddled out behind her, Clyde behind him. Then the next thing, a splash as Kirk walks right off the pier, and Clyde sees a white diaper disappearing in the dark water, the only thing he can see left of Kirk. And it was thirteen feet deep there at the end of the pier, with a big water gauge sticking out, marked like a measuring stick.

Then the next thing Melissa knows is another big splash and Clyde jumping into the water, grabbing at the baby boy fast sinking straight to the bottom.

He brought Kirk up at arm's length over his own head. And plopped him back on the pier. Soon as Kirk got a breath, he let out a mad spluttering cry and never let up the whole way back to the house. Clyde said Melissa walked along with both hands over her ears, Kirk howling and howling, dripping wet.

—I knew he would hold his breath, Clyde said. All babies know how to hold their breath. I just didn't know how long he'd hold it.

When I got back and heard this tale, I was glad Clyde had been there to rescue Kirk. Just as I was glad Rayvon had been there to change that diaper in the park shop.

9
Total Eclipse

THE DAY OF THE ECLIPSE we woke up feeling something uneasy in the air. It started getting dark around noon and the trees and bushes swelled with sudden rushing winds as if a heavy ocean swept over them. The temperature must have been dropping about ten degrees each second. I stood in front of our house, near the carved *Superintendent's Residence* sign, shivering, my arms damp and clammy, raising up hair and goose bumps. And I heard the roosters crowing across the highway in Ivory McCoy's yard.

We lived right in the path of totality. I loved the sound of that: *path of totality*. No exit. Unavoidable. We had been stamped with something special. And strange things happened all day long. People caught the biggest fish of their lives that day in Singletary Lake, or in the Cape Fear River just a few miles west. Those were fish taken out of troubled waters. There was an unfamiliar chilly shadow as people sat down to their lunch. And in the park, the

Four County Electric security light came on, triggered by the falling temperature and the surprise dusk.

Then the wind suddenly swept down on my shoulders, and I knew it was an unstoppable force because all the big Crusoe pines bowed. Together. As under a cosmic breath. I thought of those old maps with pictures of the four winds drawn into roly-poly faces, cheeks bulging and long puffs of breath blowing out on all four corners of the world.

You didn't stop that wind anymore than you stopped the sea serpents raising their long green necks in the middles of all the oceans on those old maps. It was something ancient and elemental, something without rules.

That was the solar eclipse of March 7, 1970. It started somewhere out in the Pacific Ocean south of the equator and traveled northeast at about 1,500 miles per hour across Mexico, the Gulf, across the Florida Panhandle, and on up the eastern seaboard.

The path of totality spread about eighty miles wide, northeasterly across North Carolina, and Singletary Lake Group Camp sat right in the middle. And while the total eclipse lasted for us only about three minutes, around 1:29 p.m. on a Saturday, the effect was spectacular. We would see a fiery-rimmed orb in a clear black sky flower with flames and sprout long tongues. We would feel the four winds blowing hard at the backs of our legs, our hair raised up like crowns.

One night before the eclipse, Melissa got me to come look at the full moon shining in her room. She gave me a slight scare at first. I was lying there half asleep and then Melissa appeared out of deep shadows to tug my arm.

—Mama? Come look at the moon.

We went through a sleeping house sprawled open with moonlight. The corners and gables pitched black. Everything took on high definition. A spoon and bowl left on the kitchen counter gleamed, their curves made as precise as intaglio. We had made such travels through the house before, Melissa and I in the night, Melissa a baby in my arms, me a new person just come to the strange wilderness, both of us sleepy and skittish.

And as Melissa and I prowled this rich dark, our house built out of common knotty-pine panels and red bricks, I had the notion somewhere a big quiet animal was dreaming about us and liking its dream, never wanting to wake up. The moon spotlighted a north window. Unusual to see the moon in the north. Most often it showed on the southeast side of the house, pouring down the black pines.

Melissa had wanted to share this big moon so much she'd gotten up and walked through the house without turning on a single light. Now she tugged me again as she had when waking me up. We began whispering. We didn't need talking out loud right then. Whispering was better, exchanging some soft translation of our companionship.

—See it, Mama, Melissa whispered. Mama?

—Yes, I see it. It's so big.

—It's looking right in, Mama.

We stood and admired it awhile, mother and daughter, worshipers of the mysterious and the beautiful, the ordinary and the familiar.

Then Melissa got back in bed and the white moon floated around her, up to her neck, white as flannel or snow. The curtains moved quietly and I eased back into my own half-asleep vision of the moon, dreaming *my child, her hair, her pillow. I am in love with this, with my child, the moon, this.*

I wanted the children to respect the sky and what happened in it. Got them both Little Golden Books about stars and weather, got

Kirk, Heather, and Melissa, ca. 1962

them both Petersen's field guides. And dragged them both out of their beds to look at comets. I pointed at the burning smears in the night sky.

—Look, that's a comet, I said. A million miles away.

The children weren't listening to me. I hugged them, breathed their healthy skin and hair, piquant, overpowering. Comet means long hair.

I pointed north where that starry fire-hair thinned backward.

—See! I wanted them to remember and be impressed and perhaps take comfort in such memory in their old age. Maybe they'd only remember being pulled out of bed. Going outside in the middle of the hot night and having to pee. Squirming away from the nag of my voice. Mixing up the memory with the smell of shampoo, the smell of the sandy pine woods cooling off. Their actual observation of this, I realized, would be as shadowy and unreal as the comet's long hair burning away on the horizon toward Elizabethtown.

They might remember other things. Kirk, for example, liked to burnoose himself in a flannel blanket his Grandmother Mary Lilly Miller made for him. She'd gone to the trouble to pick out a design of tough brown bronco cowboys and Indians, then crocheted little delicate white shells along the hem. He ran around making this blanket look as formidable as Superman's cape, his dark hair ruffling in the night breeze, and then settled himself for a tame ride in the wagon.

Clyde pulled him behind as we walked through Crusoe observing the summer constellations. Melissa jogged about awhile, disdaining the wagon. She liked to point out stars above the trees, listening as Clyde and I named the easy ones we knew, the good old Dipper, the belt of Orion, the gnat-swarm of the Pleiades that you had to look at sideways. Sometimes those stars looked close enough to pick, like sharply burning berries in a patch.

Soon Melissa climbed in the wagon, wrapping her arms and legs around Kirk, sharing some of the flannel blanket. He would sing something he'd learned in kindergarten about a dog: *B.I.ngo. B.I.ngo, and Bingo was his name-o.* Melissa joined in the song, and it seemed to mimic the roll of the wagon wheels down the park road, a*nd Bingo was his name-o.*

By the time we got back to the house, Clyde and I had two warm flannel lumps sleeping in a red wagon.

Once we saw a huge balloon of fire explode and shower down the darkening east, toward the Atlantic. For a while we were a bit stunned, not sure we'd actually witnessed the thing. The children wanted to know what it was.

—That's the Martians, said Clyde, coming here to get us.

The children improved on his teasing. No, it's Star Trek!

—No, Rocky and Bullwinkle!

Whatever it was, it exploded, showered fire, then vanished beyond the dark woods and surface of the lake. We went to bed, still wondering.

—It's Rocky and Bullwinkle, the children insisted, you bet?

But the next morning, nobody remembered it much. Clyde went off to work in his official park uniform, the white embroidered dogwood patch crisp on his shoulder. The children busied themselves with Lego and Lincoln Logs, Play Doh and Slinkies. And I poured another cup of coffee, not paying any attention to the television until Tom Brokaw mentioned something about a satellite launched from Cape Kennedy at sundown and aborted minutes after launch. His perfect enunciation destroyed all the pleasant fantasies. So, that's what it was last night.

I wished I hadn't heard. The spectacular fire ball was an aborted satellite. What an ugly word, *aborted*. I tried to patch it back together, our thrill, our speculation, the teasing between Clyde and the children, the flaming surprise and then the quick vanishing into the dark. Who cared about a satellite? I smacked down the cup, stirred more cream into the hot coffee and watched it swirl. *No, it's Star Trek! No, Rocky and Bullwinkle!*

For weeks, predictions and warnings about the solar eclipse had circulated in newspapers and appeared on post office walls. The North Carolina Society for the Prevention of Blindness worried about people looking directly at the eclipse and burning their retinas. The NSA Goddard Space Flight Center sent around instructions on how to make little safety devices with which to watch the eclipse indirectly. The devices were similar to pinhole cameras, or the old camera obscura often mentioned in Victorian science fiction.

Clyde cut viewing holes into the sides of cardboard boxes, just like they said. He fixed two pieces of white cardboard with a pin-hole on one. The sun would shine through the hole on one and cast a shadow on the other. We could watch the moon move across the sun and nobody's eyes would get burned.

The whole thing took on an aura of science fiction, Victorian or otherwise, as the time drew closer. You expected H. G. Wells to show up with his time machine. Astronomers and physicists and ordinary curiosity-seekers poured in from all over the United States, Stanford, Allentown, Osh Kosh. They got camping permits from Clyde and set up observation posts at Jones Lake State Park, about twelve miles from Crusoe.

One pair of astronomers, an excited husband and wife team, brought two enormous and hideous dogs on leash. The dogs sat there in the sand at Jones Lake, perfectly quiet, and gazed around at everybody with big yellow eyes, eyes like marbles, eyes you wouldn't want to run up on in the dark. They added an uncanny feeling to an already uncanny event.

After a while, the dogs just yawned and flopped down, nose to paws. They wouldn't care less when the sun turned cold and dark over their heads. And while their masters, the half-crazed astronomers, tried not to look at the alluring corona licking around the dark moon, tried not to go blind, those two dogs were going to just shut their big old yellow eyes and snore.

Clyde and I waited as eagerly as the rest of these people for Saturday, March 7, 1970. Unknown to us, Melissa had invited her fifth-grade teacher to watch the eclipse at Singletary. Melissa, at ten, was proud of her home in the woods, untidy and casual as it might seem to others. She felt she had something special to share out there. She didn't know the teacher might interpret it a bit differently.

And up the teacher drove in a smart shiny car and stepped out, dressed for tea, obviously not concerned about hiking those swampy woods to watch the sun go out. It bothered me a little.

But I got over it for Melissa's sake, and offered the teacher some humble lunch, chunky peanut butter on thick brown bread, and a mug of Clyde's special coffee. Clyde gave her a little cardboard box to view the eclipse. She seemed to relax, wobbling just a bit in her good heels, and realize the Millers were harmless. A couple of times, I believe she looked for a polite way to get back in her car and leave.

I kept the television on to make sure we didn't miss the countdown. When it started, nobody even half-alive would have missed such a thing, a total eclipse of the sun.

Exactly on cue, the moon moved toward the sun and began taking over. Clyde came out of the park office to show us the little half-moons dancing across his cardboard viewer. Like little fingernails, they dug out bigger and darker crescents from the solar ball. Melissa's teacher made polite conversation, tried to engage Melissa who had turned shy.

—Tell me the multiplication tables, giggled the teacher. I won't bite!

Melissa shrugged, yanked at Kirk until he chased her around the yard. The teacher giggled again. I knew she probably thought she'd be much better off at home in Elizabethtown in front of her own television. But there she was in the woods with us.

I peered into the viewer. Look, said Clyde. It's really happening.

And the woods turned dark. Mysterious shadowy bands of light and dark ran across the sand and into the dry oak leaves still heaped up from last winter. Thousands of little crescent lights sprinkled around us and reflected between tree limbs where new March buds had begun to swell. These were crescents reflecting from the relentless moon, broken into thousands of lights as in a prism, and scattered down on our heads, faces, spattering our hair.

A definite feeling of night. Dropped down like a curtain at the moment of total eclipse. I wanted to look directly at the sun, right at the place I'd been warned against. I wanted to see the corona's long fiery ribbons shoot through the dark craters of the moon and flame out like a monstrous sunflower. For a moment I didn't even care if I went blind.

The security light came on. And the children laughed to see it doing its job, an obedient implement triggered to illuminate all darkness, nighttime, thunderstorms, and any eclipses of the sun. The temperature dropped 20.5 degrees Fahrenheit in one hour and seventeen minutes. I read all these official measurements later in the *Raleigh News and Observer*, which also reported data collected by jet aircraft, rockets, and satellites tracking every inch of the eclipse's 8,500-mile journey over land and water.

All we knew right then at Crusoe was that it got cold and dark, and then a big wind rushed up, bringing goose bumps. Out in the swamp, black bears climbed to the tops of trees. Raccoons paced like tired nervous old men, then settled in their beds. And red foxes started grooming themselves, feeling the air cool and thicken. Ivory McCoy's chickens went to roost, tucking their heads under their wings.

Saturn, Venus, and Mercury were visible overhead as we witnessed three minutes of darkness, and everything familiar turned eerie. Melissa got quiet and huddled closer to me, slipping a hand in my jeans pocket. Kirk, usually so eager for adventure, suddenly ran back inside the house. He turned on all the lights, and we watched him run from room to room, the lights tracking his anxiety as he kept calling out, You all come inside!

Like the black bears and the foxes, like those fish taken from troubled waters, Kirk was responding to some ancient warning. We didn't know how to comfort him. So just stood outside watching the lights flick on, on, on. He paused a moment in the front door, I said you all come inside!, then ran back to turn on more lights.

It was as if he offered a sacrifice of all the lights in our house to hold the darkness at bay. And maybe somewhere else that same moment, in big stone cities or in similar backwoods, other little sacrifices were made, little prayers mumbled, and candles lit at shrines. Maybe little goldfish thrashed about in their own glassy cosmos, dreading the dark cold surprise. Everything connects.

Then it was over. As quietly as it had gone dark, the sun came back full and glorious. The little shining crescents danced to the opposite sides of our viewing boxes. The mysterious shadows banded once more, this time running in straight lines right over the sand, right over our feet. Ivory McCoy's roosters crowed. The security light flickered off. A new day.

We shook ourselves, rubbed our cold arms, and whispered as if in church. Kirk ran out of the house so relieved and so delighted, a child of sun and air, good health and plain earth. He sought to throw off the whole troubling cosmic experience by immediately teasing Melissa into a game of tag. The dog barked and rolled around us, as excited and relieved as Kirk.

I was still struck by what I'd just witnessed. A total eclipse of the sun. I'd stood right in the path of it. And three minutes of my life changed. The last such eclipse seen in our area of North Carolina had occurred on May 28, 1900. None of us had been born. The next of equal magnificence could happen on April 9, 2004. I would be sixty-five years old, if alive, in that April. Melissa would be forty-four and Kirk forty-one. Clyde and the dog could both be dead. And the fifth-grade schoolteacher could still be wondering why she spent her Saturday in those woods.

The black bears, the raccoons, and the red foxes, even Ivory McCoy's chickens would again climb to the tops of the trees, or pace in circles, groom themselves, then quietly tuck their heads down and sleep through it.

10
Weathering

THE WEATHER BREWED UP CLOSE to Clyde and me in the woods. A sudden showering of clear hard rain sprang across the yard and then was gone, leaving deep little pits in the sand that dried in a heartbeat. Leaving a fresh woodsy smell you did not get even from grass or new-cut hayfields. Frost traveled through the brown turkey oaks in the dead of November turning every leaf white as a spider web. And you could smell snow coming a long way off in January.

But the thunderstorms of early summer were the best. They formed and dissolved—*decayed*, the weatherman said on TV—rapidly. First Clyde and I got strong winds rippling the tops of the big pines, then fierce lightning, then the heavy downpours, a thick white rush of water flooding the roof and making long flat pools across the park roads, seeming deeper because of the dark asphalt. And then—just as rapidly—the storms vanished.

I liked the smell of summer rain on the wild blueberry thickets. I picked baskets of ripe blueberries with the children starting in late May. Commercial blueberries are harvested earlier in coastal Carolina, but the wild ones continue to set berries and ripen on into June, sometimes into July, making the air fragrant and intoxicating every flying insect within range.

Thus it was best to pick berries right after a hard rain, the mosquitoes and yellow jackets being too soggy to challenge us then. Still I soaked strips of rags in turpentine and tied them around every wrist and ankle, sprayed every neck and face with repellent, before we dared invade those sweet-smelling bogs across the road from the house.

The wild berries were irregular in shape and color but never in flavor. Pale blue to a deep purple almost velvety black, they filled the baskets and left stains on our hands and mouths. Eventually, the rain dried off the bushes and the mosquitoes clouded back to sting right through the turpentine and strong repellent. The children and I dashed out of the woods, hosed off in the yard, washing ourselves and the berries. The next day I made thick sweet blueberry jam, packing it into glass jars and sealing each with a pale crown of paraffin. I always figured I had enough to last until winter. But we could not resist. One by one the paraffin crowns were lifted and the jam spooned out on toast, pancakes, peanut-butter sandwiches. Each bite tasted as fresh and wild and surprising as June thunderstorms, as satisfying as watching lightning from a safe place.

We did not save the wild honey the bees made behind the rough plankings of the group camp mess hall. A hive had wintered there. Gone unnoticed and undisturbed until the next spring. Then their flights and swarmings got Rayvon Kinlaw and other park workers upset.

—Law', declared Rayvon, I'd ruther be snake bit than bee bit. And then all of them said they wouldn't work down in the group camp until the bees were gone.

So Clyde got a beekeeper from down at Lagoon to deal with the bees. The man first thought he could tear off the planking and get the queen in a box and the rest of the swarm would follow. But the hive was far bigger and more elaborate than anyone had imagined. Its combs spread over and around and through the side of the mess hall in a spectacular labyrinth of wax and dark thick honey.

The beekeeper decided to smoke the bees, hoping to salvage a portion of the honey. He swung his smudge pots, like old-fashioned oil cans with long spouts, and the bees roared inside the wall and flew out, then drooped and fell.

Rayvon and the other men pulled off the plankings and scraped the honeycombs into washtubs, dead bees stuck all over. They stuck their fingers in the honey, tasted, spat it back out. Too strong, they pronounced. You might could eat it, said Rayvon, but awful strong.

I stuck in a finger and the wild smoked honey flooded my tongue. They were right. Too strong and thick, and hard to swallow. Still, I wished we could keep it, pick off the dead bees, the crushed comb, pour it into big glass jars and keep it for a cold winter evening. The wild flavors of bees and smoke would surely comfort us. We would be fed.

The idea of being both wild and safe in the same place appealed to me, of being a natural part of this wilderness and yet a tame observer. I considered all its seasons and its weather my own, and all its creatures, too.

I kept a small bike and often rode it alone when the children were in school and Clyde away. The steady exercise cleared my thoughts after hours of wrestling with words on a page. One autumn afternoon I rode my bike to the spillway and discovered a big blue heron. The dog trotting along with me dashed ahead to drink and flushed him. The big heron was feeding in the waterfall and surprised me as he rose up, his wings making a rushing sound. He was the color of blue slate, all alone, no other birds with him. I watched him rise to the tops of the trees, then settle slowly onto a branch. He comforted me somehow, as if a wild calendar turned as steadily as my bike wheels in the sand.

The black bear I saw the next morning did not offer the same comfort to me, at least not at first. We had seen bear tracks in the sand often, usually where one had walked through the group camp, none close to the house. Black bears were known to be shy, hurrying off to vanish in the blueberry bogs when they heard people approach. I'd never heard of anyone in Bladen County who actually encountered a black bear face to face, except when hunting one. And they could be hunted.

I was alone in the Beetle, driving Kelly Star Route toward town, and as I came upon the small opening in the pond bay and underbrush, right at the curve of the road where you first glimpse the bright flash of Singletary Lake, I noticed an unusually big black dog. Big as a calf, I thought. Husky, maybe, and very shaggy. A husky dog probably just burning up in the Bladen heat.

Then as I got about parallel with the husky dog, he stood up and he was taller than my car. And he was a black bear, just looking, just waiting for me to get on by. There are not many times when my mouth falls open, but it did then. I didn't dare slow for a better look. I chugged on by. The bear stood with his front paws folded on his chest, like some old man, blinking in the sun.

In my rear mirror, I watched him drop to all fours, amble across the road.

A bear! I saw a bear!

This really scared me. Then the scare melted and a deep immense thrill took its place. I saw a wild bear. Alone. He made me feel sought out. And so it was with genuine regret the next hunting season that I saw the shaggy carcasses of two dead black bears in the bed of a pick-up parked in Elizabethtown. People gathered to gawk at them. The hunters lifted up the bears' heads. Their heavy tongues dangled out and made them look silly.

Again I felt sought out. And given something to tell people. Late in October that year, a warm hazy and fragrant Sunday, Clyde and I took the children to play on pine-straw bales stacked up under trees on the side of Singletary fronting Kelly Star Route. Bladen Lakes State Forest baled the straw for mulch and it smelled ripe and tangy, like pine rosin, but not at all sticky. Melissa and Kirk climbed the stacks, jumped off, climbed up again. There were dozens of bales, all across from where I saw the first black bear of my life.

—What if that bear comes out here again? I said, chewing a sprig of pine straw. It tasted spicy, almost the way good tobacco smells.

Clyde smiled. Well, he said, how fast can you get up to the top of those bales?

People came to Singletary Lake Group Camp and did things to it. Fish biologists had two powerful ways to make fish counts. In one, they submerged a pole and sent out small electrical shocks several feet in a circle. The fish floated to the surface and got counted. The men drifted around in those fiberglass boats and simply pointed one, two, three.

They said the shocks were harmless, that fish didn't really feel anything. But how could they tell? I watched from the pier feeling the air crisp as autumn around us. Gray moss festooned the cypresses along the shore. I saw the fish glint on the dark water for a second before they fluttered, flipped over and submerged.

It nagged at me. Maybe fish hated sudden shocks, those numbing electrical circles that reached deep into the cold silence of Singletary water and pushed them to the surface. And they fluttered helpless and scared, the bright alien air flooding upon them.

In the second way to make fish counts, the men used a paralyzing drug called roetnone. Roetnone came from South American leguminous plants called cubé. The natives had always used it, crushing the leaves and roots, then dropping them into the water to paralyze the fish and make an easy catch. Now cubé was distilled and concentrated into a liquid almost pure roetnone. This liquid dropped in Singletary Lake paralyzed all fish and other aquatic life instantly. The fish floated up to the surface again and were counted by the men in fiberglass boats. Roetnone, too, they said was perfectly harmless, fish didn't feel a thing.

They knew exactly how many red fin and gar and horned catfish swam through the dark water, as well as turtles and snakes and frogs and crawdads. A miracle anything could live in such dark and acid water. Sunlight did not penetrate Singletary to any great depth, so very few plants grew on the peaty bottom for fish to feed on.

Little black eels swam up Colly Creek and through the peripheral swamps to get into the lake. Nobody figured out just how they did that. Eels were long snakelike fish who migrated from freshwater to spawn in the Sargasso Sea. Then the young ones struggled back to freshwater again. Somehow those ugly black eels got all the way back to Bladen County from an island of seaweed floating between the West Indies and the Azores. Got back to Colly Creek a few miles below our house, and then into our dark lake. Perhaps the blue heron ate them. Perhaps he remembered each year. Perhaps the black bear I saw had eels in mind as he crossed the road. Their wild unseen calendar moved to its own rhythm.

One cold spring the campgrounds were busy with biology students who went nuts when it began to rain one night in torrents. They'd discovered Singletary Lake Group Camp overrun with a certain kind of frog that only mated during a downpour. They slopped around all night shining flashlights and scooping up frogs in plastic buckets. I wanted to know what they were going to do with all those frogs.

—Play with them. Look at them. Learn things. Clyde brushed the rain off his hat.

—Like what things?

—Frog things. He went back out, the rain like steel needles.

—Like what! I followed to the screen door and held it open past the drip line.

—Like sex, he said, frog sex.

The same downpour overflowed the lake and flooded Colly Creek. Water flew over the little dam in hard white spray. A day or two after the big frog-mating storm, I stood with the children by the spillway looking at dozens of big catfish poking their heads out of the water to gasp air. The poor fish tossed around by the heavy rain washed up Colly Creek and got trapped in a pool beside the dam. When the rain stopped and the creek receded, the catfish had no exit. Now they smothered to death. Enough water to swim up the creek. But not enough to breathe.

Clyde got a net and we scooped some over the dam into the lake. We got sopping wet, the children muddy. I didn't like catfish, never had liked those horns and slimy skins. But now I felt sorry for them.

Most of the fish were more scared of the net than of smothering, so they fled to the bottom of the pool and hid. Those fish died. They floated up to the surface and did not revive from this shock as their fellows had from the electricity and the roetnone.

Two geologists from Williams College came to collect core samples of the pollen in Singletary Lake. Those samples would be examined by other geologists back at Williams who could then determine what kinds of vegetation grew around the lake thousands of years ago.

The men worked from a raft and took samples from various areas and depths of the lake bed. Their equipment looked like a miniature oil-drilling rig. Clyde and I watched them drift around the water, pausing to sink long metal tubes, then withdraw each carefully. The cores were extremely fragile, bored right out of the prehistoric past. The men turned them out on newspapers spread over the floor of the camp infirmary, the only place wide enough to accommodate them. The naked samples looked like long tubes of multicolored sand. The ancient pollen remained invisible, but definitely bound among the peat and other debris.

Pollen seemed such a delicate, almost ephemeral thing. The yellow dust shaking out of flowers, pale as ashes sometimes, with a touch like butterfly wings. How could they really find it?

The geologists, sunburned by their long days on the lake, told us some of the samples from Singletary were 10,000 years old. In Massachusetts, somebody could separate that old pollen from the

Melissa at the spillway, 1964

sand and read it, identify it as Pleistocene, Precambrian. The giant conifers and ferns of ancient swamps would reassemble, seed and spore, gene, chromosome. And the other lives of my amazing Crusoe's Island would be revealed.

They dropped by the park house to share a beer and sit on the brick steps out front and tell Clyde these things. The core samples were fragile as sand castles our children made by packing wet sand in plastic pails and then turning them over to dry in the hot sun. One kick, and the castles were gone. How to transport such things, I asked the geologists?

—A pinch here, a pinch there, they said. And they took scrapings all along the long tube of material. Labeling each pinch, each scrape, then packing it all and sending up to Williams College. Dozens of photographs, too, carefully labeled and analyzed.

Such fine powder from the anthers of plants, the sex life of the Jurassic age: those wet core samples, like the frogs, the eels, the dark fish in the lake, had to be numbered and examined and written up in reports.

And somewhere in the background, a blue heron, a black bear, wild berries and bees and thunderstorms went on without fail.

11
Some Calling Birds

IN THE MIDDLE OF A WARM AND colorful October, goldenrod blooming over road banks and persimmons ripening, a pigeon appeared at our house. He wore a band on one leg and behaved so calmly, fearing nobody, we figured he was someone's pet. A carrier pigeon, homing pigeon, or racing pigeon, we didn't know. But he did have the band on him. He had been handled by people for something.

Kirk was especially pleased when the pigeon walked up and down the road beside him. He wouldn't let Kirk touch him, always fluttering just beyond reach. But he did follow Kirk and nobody else. At dusk, he went to roost in the rafters of the garage, making a cozy warm blur up there in the dark, his smooth white head tucked down.

Kirk wanted to know why the pigeon did that, putting a wing over his head. Clyde said it was the pigeon's covers, the same as people pulled blankets up to their chins. Or to make it dark and sleep-like.

The pigeon stayed at Crusoe a week, strutting through the edge of the woods, pecking seeds, leaving the faintest tracks in the sand, dim little crosshatches. Every afternoon, Kirk got off the school bus and ran to the house looking for him. The pigeon kept close to the boy. Kirk thought he was his. Then one weekend, in the sudden peaking of the fall, he vanished.

Kirk moped around awhile. Then, I reckon he's gone home, he told us, my little pigeon. But he always kept looking for the pigeon to come back.

He rescued birds from the two black cats, even one with a broken beak. The bird could still fly and his heart beat so hard, I saw the speckled breast feathers move. Kirk brought it in on the porch and it flew around, knocking into the screens. Then he took it back out, opened his hands, and it flew off into the woods.

He tried to hatch a small pink egg he found lying on the sand near the park gate. No nest in the trees, and none in the bushes, so Kirk nested the egg in his old Easter basket with a hot water bottle and a woolly toboggan. After a few days, I suggested it might not hatch, and maybe he ought to throw the egg away.

Kirk poked at the Easter basket, tested the hot water bottle, unfolded the toboggan. The egg looked like a pink marble, a jelly bean.

—It was already cold when I found it, he admitted.

—It might not hatch, then.

—Just one more day.

One more day, and the pink egg still didn't hatch. So Kirk got rid of all his incubator stuff. He really wanted that egg to hatch, to raise the chick, whatever it turned out to be.

I could tell he was still trying to bring back the pigeon.

The next Easter, Clyde brought him and Melissa some dyed biddies from the FCX. Knots of blue and pink fluff, the biddies cheeped and pecked and slept as if drugged on the front porch. Then died, just keeled over in the middle of their pecking, closed their eyes, and passed away.

It happened while the children were at school, so Clyde got the things buried before they could come home to find cold fluff in the box on the porch. Kirk didn't seem too mournful this time, just sort of shook his head over the dumb fates of FCX biddies. Clyde tried to tell him how hard it was to raise chickens. Chickens were a complicated science. You needed vitamins and antibiotics and appetite enhancers and growth stimulators.

Kirk said he just wanted the biddies to go out in the yard and scratch and peck and run around and live to be big old granddaddy chickens.

Ivory McCoy's chickens were free-range white Leghorns. And when Ivory wanted one to eat, he wrung its neck. Grabbed one up still squawking and casually slung it in a wide circle over his head, the feathers flying like snow, until its neck stretched.

Then Regina or Omega or Elise but certainly never Loretta *(Loretta, she don't like them damn chickens)*, plunged it into boiling water, squatted in the sand and picked off all the feathers.

My grandmother, the jolly and pretty and gentle-spoken Jennie Ross, used to kill chickens with a little hatchet, strike off their heads with one hard blow. Their headless bodies flapped all over the garden, spattering blood, their hard yellow legs running, running. Her chickens were free-range Dominiques, what they called Domineckers, finely speckled black and white, with a rosy comb. She always killed at least two at a time for Sunday dinner. And she was still lithe enough at sixty to squat and pick and singe both chickens without getting a cramp or a twinge of arthritis.

But the killing of chickens was nothing. A necessary task, what a woman did to get Sunday dinner, set her family down to heavy platters of the succulent golden breast pieces, the crisp legs, the rich gravy ladled over creamy potatoes. Spilling blood was only part of this feasting.

Other killings were other things, however. I could tell the story. Of being about six years old, old enough to go to school, and still loving to visit long lazy days and nights with my favorite grandmother in the country in summer. One morning I woke earlier than usual, padded downstairs barefoot, out the long central hall. Nobody was in the house. I went to the kitchen. My place was set for breakfast, the bowl ready for oatmeal, the sugar at hand, and on the back of the stove, my spoon kept warm in a pan of water. A loving and special touch. Nobody else ever warmed a spoon for me.

I slipped out the back door, crossed the barnyard and saw Jennie huddled over something in the garden. Her cotton sunbonnet had slipped from her head and bobbed on her back like a print-sprigged knapsack.

—Grandmother! I approached with joy. The garden dirt already warm underfoot. It would be another hot day. Grandmother!

Jennie Ross turned slowly, seemed to be hiding something in front of her. But I'd already seen, coming closer, still calling, Grandmother!

Three kittens floated in a washtub. Jennie still held a fourth under the water. I stopped short, put a finger in my mouth. What're you doing to those kitties, I asked.

Grandmother Jennie Ross didn't say anything for a while. Then, I'm putting them to sleep, she said. They have to go to sleep.

When my mother came to collect me later in the afternoon, Jennie told her the story. I heard her declare, I wouldn't have done it for the world if I'd known she'd be there watching. Not for the world. I turned around and she was just standing there with her finger in her mouth.

—It's okay, said my mother, who didn't like such confessions, who tried to back away from such. You can't keep every cat in the world.

Later I could not remember if I really saw this or if I only dreamed it. My mother shook her head at any mention of it, shushing me up. But I thought it up again through so many years, now with Kirk and Melissa and all those Easter biddies. My gentle grandmother who kept spoons warm. Who maybe had killed the kittens. And maybe had let me see it.

Kirk never raised any free-range chickens at Singletary Lake Group Camp. And the pigeon never came back.

I got stopped by highway patrolmen checking licenses and tags one winter afternoon and was late getting to Elizabethtown Primary School to pick Kirk up. I hurried along under a sky so clear blue, it almost dazzled. The air was sharp from the last snow which still lay around in hard glassy patches. The schoolyard was deserted. Kirk sat alone on the steps, his books toppling to one side, both arms clasped around his knees to keep warm.

—When you didn't come soon, he whispered, I was afraid you'd been *slaughtered*.

I wondered where he'd picked up a word like that, slaughtered.

—Nobody slaughtered me, honey, I said, thinking it sounded reassuring.

He got in the car and held his hands to the heat vents. I sat there so long, Mama, the birds hopped up to me. I might could've touched those birds on the head.

His anxiety over my lateness seemed matched by his wonder at being able to get close to the birds. Things like that impress a boy living in the woods, even if you had to go to school everyday in Elizabethtown. Shortening the distance between you and the wilderness, being able almost to touch birds on the head was a triumph. And not to be taken for granted.

The next summer, Kirk got an even bigger triumph. We often went along when Clyde went up to Raleigh on state park business. On the Capitol Square, there was a famous old Peanut Man. He sold thousands of bags of parched peanuts to people who then fed them to the pigeons flocking around. A good-humored old fellow, he never said much, just sold the peanuts and watched what you did with the pigeons.

That morning he gave Kirk a free bag of peanuts, then put his finger to his lips, Shhh.

Kirk grinned and began shelling and feeding peanuts and soon he was covered up with greedy pigeons, some waddling around his feet, others perching on his shoulders and head, all of them flapping their wings and making that pleasant humming sound, not so much a sound of cooing as a babbling underwater.

Kirk seemed transfixed, a boy of birds and wings. They came to his hands and he dispensed blessings right and left, generous as St. Francis. The old Peanut Man had picked him out. There were dozens of other little boys around the Capitol that day, but only Kirk commanded wild birds.

Melissa and I stood back, already planning how to tell it to Clyde when we were going home in the car at evening. And I knew, I felt deep in my bones, too, that someday, when I was one hundred years old, Kirk was going to call me up and say, I was remembering the pigeons today.

Clyde enjoyed fixing the children's breakfast in little individual servings. Each place set with blue, yellow, or brown pottery bowls, each bowl with its teaspoon. They trooped into the dining room and found he had sweet applesauce, buttered grits, scrambled eggs in the bowls and buttered toast cut in half stacked on saucers. A small shot glass of juice for each. They liked it and he liked doing it. And while I never thought of doing such a thing, it did make me think of my Grandmother Jennie warming spoons for oatmeal.

I would sit there sipping coffee, remembering the good times at her house, remembering, in inevitable sequence, the shock of the drowned kittens.

And I wondered indeed what these two children might remember of me, of their father, and this place in the woods. Pigeons, yes, Easter biddies, yes, and maybe the harsh word *slaughtered* in some curious context of dread and comfort.

12
Paratroopers

Veteran paratroopers jumped into Singletary Lake. They had been injured and couldn't risk jumps onto hard ground or pavement. But water was okay. So they got permission to jump into the lake. That way they could get in enough hours to draw their jump pay and also avoid further injuries.

The helicopters roared down from Fort Bragg to the north, and the men began jumping out. Parachutes billowed behind them, and then they plopped into the dark water. I was allowed to stand on the pier and watch along with miscellaneous military persons and the jumpers' families. Clyde and some rangers paddled around in the rowboats with poles and life rings, just in case.

A reckless affirmation of faith, men flinging themselves out of whizzing helicopters hovering over the lake like monster dragonflies. Falling and hitting the water and floating there awhile, laughing at each other, and cursing good-naturedly.

The first day of these maneuvers, Clyde picked the children up early from school so they could see it. On the way home, they stopped at Wam Squam, their favorite filling station near White Lake—the odd name meant White Water—and got a drink and some crackers. Kirk also got a Secret Agent Watch that launched plastic bullets by spring action right off his wrist, and he tormented his sister with it.

At Singletary, in the white cleared space between the lake and the spillway, the first helicopters were gunning up, and some of the troopers invited Kirk to go up with them. I started to protest, but he climbed on inside and sat down, his Secret Agent Watch primed to fire. Then he took a look at his companions. Seasoned veterans of both war and peace, tough guys with real beards, G.I. Joes of the first caliber, gutta percha kneecaps and steel pins in their hipbones. Kirk stared. They looked back with a benign detachment. He was eight years old and suddenly not too sure about this deal. A plastic bullet from Wam Squam meant nothing here.

Then the boss, a sergeant or something meaner, ran over and yelled that the kid couldn't go up, too dangerous, so, get that kid outta there! Kirk jumped back out, his Keds sliding in the sand, both disappointed and relieved. The helicopters took off. The blades whizzed and whined and carried the men far out over Singletary Lake and they routinely jumped out.

Like the fish coming to the surface to be counted, propelled by shock or roetnone, those men floated in big circles and waited to be picked up by other men in boats, all of them wearing heavy combat boots and backpacks, their exotic military gear hanging off their bodies like surreal tool belts. They just tumbled out of the loud bellies of the helicopters without a care or a thought, splashing right into the long flat cola-colored lake.

Toward the end of that day, a few of the paratroopers missed the lake and ended up across Kelly Star Route in the turkey oaks, landing near the settlement of Ivory McCoy and his strange family of women. Ivory's people had lived forever either on the park or in Bladen Lakes State Forest. They held claim to the sandy woods through something stronger and more binding than common squatters' rights: the long patient claim of sheer survival. Clyde remained on good terms with Ivory. In a real forest fire or some similar disaster, only Ivory would know the trails back through the trees and across the swamps. Only Ivory could save people.

Ivory and his women were alarmed by the sight of all those white men falling out of helicopters, some disappearing in an orange mushroom of parachute over the trees and into Singletary, still others crashing right down in their yards.

—Godamighty! they said, Bless Jesus! And they approached the paratroopers with caution, Say, where you come from? Who your daddy be?

The jumpers, who weren't hurt or the slightest bit apprehensive, explained where they came from. Ivory said they never saw no white men falling out of no airplanes before. He crossed the road with the jumpers who had to catch the military vans back to Bragg.

—Captain, Ivory asked Clyde, how come white people want to go fall out of airplanes?

—I don't know. Because they want to.

Ivory mused on this awhile standing in the yard. Well, he said, I guess they know what they be wantin.

Ivory and his people, as isolated as Clyde and I in the wilderness of Bladen County, sometimes wanted to talk to the outside world. They had radio and television, but no telephone. One afternoon not long after the spectacle of the paratroopers, Ivory and Loretta, accompanied by old Regina and the two sisters, Omega and Elise, drove up outside.

Loretta sat with a child in her arms. Only Regina emerged from the car, a dark imperious energy, making her slow determined way down the walk to us on the porch.

—Tyrone, she said to Clyde through the screen door, the baby, he be sick. He be the baby.

She turned back toward the car and gave a sweep of her arm. They all be babies, Captain, but Tyrone, he be sick.

She pointed directly at the child in Loretta's arms. Loretta looked neither to the right nor the left. Omega, whose grandchild that was, said nothing, but stared from the backseat among the other children.

Regina continued, And we want you to go call up Daddy Armstrong out in Los Anga*lees*, California, Captain, and ask him to pray for Tyrone.

Regina squinted at Clyde, at me and the children sitting on the porch listening. Sunlight fingered the trees and tinged Regina's hair which wasn't braided in Loretta's dreadlocks, not even brushed up like the children's Brillo. Regina's hair was powdery gray and gathered back from her head in a knot right over her collar.

She smoothed the knot for emphasis. You do that, Captain? You go call up Daddy Armstrong out in Los Anga*lees*, California?

The telephone, whether in the house or over in Clyde's office, like everything else in the park, belonged to the State of North Carolina. It wasn't a public convenience, and Regina and Ivory accepted that.

—We pay you for it, Captain, Ivory offered. He got out of the car for his own emphasis. You go call up the man and we pay you for it. He didn't, however, want to put through the call himself. We pay you, Captain.

—I can't do that, Clyde said. I can't take money from you for the phone.

—We give you something, then, Captain. You go call up the man.

Clyde figured he could show the long-distance call as a personal call to his brother in Playa Del Rey, and so made it, directing them all over to the park office where they'd have more privacy.

Clyde got the faith-healer in California on the line and, with Regina and Ivory standing by, asked him to pray for Tyrone out in the car. Daddy Armstrong wouldn't promise any healing or praying or anything until somebody guaranteed him some money, that money to be sent immediately by a United States Postal money order.

Clyde relayed this to Regina and Ivory. They blinked a moment.

—Tell him we be sending fifty dollars, Captain.

Clyde returned to the phone. His fifty dollars guaranteed, Daddy Armstrong then told Clyde to tell the people to bring the sick child to the phone so he could breathe on him through the wires.

Ivory and Regina got Tyrone out of Loretta's arms and out of the car and into the park office and held him to the receiver. They didn't want to hold the receiver themselves, so Clyde held it against Tyrone's ear, and the breathing out in California began.

Tyrone did not respond. He lay in Regina's arms, one bare foot poking Ivory, his ear against the official telephone belonging to the State of North Carolina, Division of State Parks, Singletary Lake Group Camp, and kept his eyes shut tight. Clyde couldn't hear a thing going on in the phone. Nobody could except Tyrone. And Tyrone was too sick to say.

After a while, Clyde judged the breathing out in California ought to be done, and he took the receiver from Tyrone's ear and put it to his own. There was nothing. Dead silence. The son of a bitch in California had hung up.

Nevertheless, Ivory and Regina were grateful and satisfied. They drove off with the sick child, convinced he would wake up healed the next day, or the next. Tyrone, the same age and size as Clyde's own son.

In the late fall, after the first hard frost, Ivory brought us a car trunk full of sweet potatoes, firm and aromatic, not a single one frostbitten or bitter. I thought about Tyrone each time I baked a pan full of those potatoes, so sweet the syrup bubbled through their skins.

The paratroopers from Fort Bragg also dropped dummies in the woods around the house. To practice their retrieval and rescue operations. Also to watch them fall, studying the wind velocity, and then measuring how quickly a man could be found after falling.

They left those things just lying around in the woods after they were gone. But when I came upon them, I expected them to roll over and hold out their arms, beseeching my help, the wind riffling the trees overhead. They looked so real, so spooky and human. The children were afraid of them, and dreaded to stumble over an arm or a leg, a whole man.

What was war doing in our place? In those remote woods garlanded in Spanish moss and sunlight falling as softly as wisps of pale hair. Things so delicate and natural, you hated the cheap military games. The phony invasions. And the mindless dummies, like great big G.I. Joe dolls with broken plastic noses peeling off, fingers contorted, and eyes staring up from the ground or through a clump of bushes.

Melissa and Kirk wouldn't touch them. Too eerie. They found them everywhere those days, across the spillway muddied by the swamp, or hidden under healthy red broom straw, obscene and ungainly things disturbing everybody's peace and dignity. The dog always growled.

These things happened to us and to Ivory McCoy and gave us a kind of bond we could feel but not call its name. Daddy Armstrong and the dummy casualties, Los Anga*lees* and paratroopers. We tried to help each other out, making the phone calls, explaining the helicopters. Our two young sons, Kirk and Tyrone, standing in sometimes like the purest of offerings for gods way off in the distance where machines roared and injured men limped to war.

13
Invasions

One April, the air still raw with leftover winter wind, Easter weekend promised a pleasant blue sky and strong hot sun. Melissa helped me bake a cardamom braid, and Kirk helped me with a carrot cake. She liked crushing the aromatic seeds over the dough, and he liked grating the carrots and licking the sweet batter out of the bowl. On Good Friday, we went to the egg-hunt at Lagoon Baptist Church, about five miles down Kelly Star Route. Lagoon was actually a lookout tower for Bladen Lakes State Forest. A little community sprouted around it.

Melissa and Kirk carried brown wicker baskets and added their dyed eggs to the general supply to be hidden and shared. Most of the other children came with brown paper bags and had decorated their eggs with crayons. There were not many children, a scattering who rode the school bus into Elizabethtown each morning. Ivory McCoy and Loretta did not appear with their brood. No Tyrone. The family of Miss Burma Murdoch made up

Melissa with a friend at the Lagoon Baptist Church, Easter 1964

the bulk of the congregation at Lagoon, a jolly lady who also ran the only general store and post office in the area. She directed the egg hunt from a chair, making sure the prize egg got stuck high in the fork of a tree, and that there was plenty of candy for all.

I wondered if the children of Ivory McCoy and Loretta ever went to an egg hunt. If they, perhaps, hid in the turkey oaks like ghosts and watched. It made the egg hunt all the more exotic at

Lagoon. Brown paper bags, eggs colored with wax crayons, hidden eyes watching from the woods.

On Easter Sunday morning, Kirk called me to the backyard. Melissa stood by the big lobelia bush, holding out her right hand. A swallowtail, the first of the season had lit on her hand and sat flexing its wings. She stood so carefully, smiling at the butterfly, yellow and black wings, tiny feet and antennae.

—It tickles, she said. And then it fluttered off, maybe propelled by the slight disturbance of her breath. The perfect Easter thing.

A mosquito-fogging truck came out to the park and sprayed DDT all over the public use areas, group camp, lake front, pier, spillway, and around our house, the park maintenance shops, and Clyde's office. It was an ordinary public service in those days, the late '60s and early '70s, something to protect park users from malaria and yellow fever and other pestilence bred in the bowels of mosquitoes swarming the pocosins.

DDT, the perfect pesticide, was mixed with kerosene or diesel oil to make trillions of sticky droplets then sprayed in billowing white clouds, coating every green leaf, stem, and twig in the park. Dichlorodiphenyltrichloroethane, first concocted in 1939, my birth year, a chlorinated hydrocarbon, was good for killing things that bite and suck or eat up the vegetation. Especially good for killing in the middle of the night, the very best time to get blood-sucking mosquitoes.

The truck came out from Elizabethtown and sprayed a mist so thick and white that big floodlights were used in the place of regular headlights just to see the road. Our children, their summer pajamas fluttering, dashed barefoot out of the house and pedaled their bikes behind the truck, right through the big white clouds, frolicking and breathing huge gulps of that faintly sweet mist, pure DDT, the perfect killer.

Clyde and I should have known better. But we didn't. And so up and down the park roads, the truck made at least a dozen passes, the white stuff pouring out in all directions and those moony headlights glared. The night bugs stopped screeching. Everything got still. Everything smelling sweet and rotten, stifled on DDT. But nobody said a thing about poison or cancer or dying. Nobody had on a mask. Not me, not Clyde, not the man driving the truck. And certainly not the two children, half-naked, happy as pups chasing down the roads behind the mosquito-fogging truck.

All we thought about was killing mosquitoes. I coughed and my face tingled. My eyes stung and my lips numbed. I thought maybe my tongue swelled a little. And when I crawled back in bed, my cotton nightgown gave off a faint essence of DDT.

The stuff was poison, but everybody said it was okay. Pure DDT in the dark night air. That happened at least three summers during the thirteen years Clyde and I lived there. Then in 1973, it stopped. DDT was judged a toxic hazard and banned forever in the United States, though its manufacture continued and it was exported in tons to Third World countries. Down in Bladen County, along Colly Creek and through the Crusoe's Island swamps, the mosquitoes swarmed back with yellow flies and deer flies, humped-back crickets and candle moths.

Maybe my body tissues flaunted radioactive DDT. As did those of the children. Years hence, getting my finger nicked for blood tests, getting routine X-rays, some curious pathological findings will darken the slides and contaminate the film. Our central nervous systems will convulse. Surely it is significant. In the middle of some future summer night, we will sicken and die. And the DDT did it.

People often asked me, How can you stand it out here?

They joked, Singletary? That ought to be *Solitary!*

One of my aunts visited and said, How come you stay in these woods? My girls wouldn't stay in these woods. My girls wouldn't stay in these woods fifteen minutes.

Clyde had asked me the same sorts of thing in the very beginning, when we first got married on a snowy Valentine's Day, and when we first got there, right before a warm and balmy Christmas.

Except he asked, Do you think you can stand this?

His was the more apt question. Not how *do* you, but do you *think* you can? He had put the responsibility squarely on me. He wanted me to respond to the demands of such isolation emotionally and thoughtfully. Will you live through it with me, is what Clyde had asked. Will you live through my dying?

He meant it as a warning and as a full commitment. He didn't want our life in the woods to be something we just lived through indifferently, or something we just *stood.*

But it was the kind of life, marriage and family, that you truly understood only if you actually lived it. It had dark sides and crazy sides, foolish moments, bitter moments, and those moments that were breathtaking and beyond ordinary testimony.

Our isolation was real. We lived in the middle of thousands of acres of trees and tried to raise two modern children in the face of such consequences—that beautiful and wild cola-dark lake, that deadly pocosin with its cypress and moss, its fur and fang and claw.

Things happened, and I wanted to get them down, either by writing stories or by making pictures with the Exakta camera. I wanted to be able to hold Crusoe in my hands. Be able to go back to it. And then, maybe, figure it out.

The cold December woods were crisp as bone with a scrubbed blue sky, that wide scrubbed clear sky I'd come to associate with the coastal lands, one morning I took the children in to school. Close to the road in some low turkey oak brush and across from the lake, an old hunting dog waited, his tongue lolling out. He watched the world out of patient brown old-dog eyes, an old friend waiting for his people to come pick him up and take him home.

He stood too close to the road, trusted too much. When I came back, he had been killed. Not more than fifteen minutes, and there he sprawled, his head knocked to one side, the sand darkening under him.

Later that spring, a big doe jumped at the yellow Ghia convertible, slamming herself against the driver's side, then somehow rebounding and sliding across the hood and into a ditch on the other side of the road. She struggled to her feet and covered about twenty yards, then fell and stayed down.

Clyde, driving the Ghia alone that morning, said she came out of nowhere on the stretch of highway between White Lake and Elizabethtown, just past Wam Squam. He turned back to Wam Squam and called the Wildlife people. They shot the doe and took her off. She couldn't be saved, but somebody could eat her. It was the Wildlife people's custom to donate a fresh and healthy animal to charity.

The damage to the Ghia was considerable, a caved-in door, dented hood, and smashed side mirror. Clyde was lucky to escape with no more than a harsh scare and some sore muscles. Another man driving in coastal Carolina that year got impaled on the antlers of a deer that, like the Bladen County doe, came out of nowhere and struck his car.

These are the things that happen in the woods. They are the moments that make life so undeniably yours, for good or for ill.

Two months later, June began a rather eerie summer for us in the park. For the first time, the entire group camp was rented for a few weeks by a philanthropical and social service organization from Raleigh. The cabins were full of delinquent boys. They shot baskets, sang around campfires, dived off the pier into Singletary Lake, fished and went boating. They looked scrubbed with Ivory soap. They devoured charcoaled hamburgers, and ran around camp wearing cut-offs and tees and high-tops as any other group would, weaving lanyards and stringing beads. They swigged dozens of Coca-Colas and looked like plain ordinary healthy boys.

Except these little boys had killed people. They had laid violent hands upon mamas and daddies, upon little sisters and brothers, upon total strangers at the mall. They knew how to use guns and knives, tire irons and chains. I thought about it, piling the briquettes in my own grill from Western Auto, patting out the hamburgers for my own children vaccinated and educated by the state.

What moved a child to commit murder?

Then I forgot about it, the way people do. For all I knew, the delinquents in the camp could be plotting my own murder. They plotted, instead, escape.

Kirk, out behind the shop playing with his plastic weapons and army surplus gear, canteen, camouflage helmet, wormed along the ground on his belly. Vulnerable at any moment to enemy attack, he suddenly saw three boys run like crazy through the woods. Their legs pumped over the old brown pine needles and tore the fresh June bay leaves.

Kirk froze. Watched. They were three of the delinquents, and he knew what that meant. He'd heard Clyde talk about it enough. They didn't see Kirk, and so headed off toward the highway, obviously not knowing where they were and having no idea which way to run.

Kirk then scrambled to the park office to report this reconnaissance mission. The boys were later picked up by the Bladen County sheriff trudging along toward Elizabethtown. The worst possible direction for escape. Not having enough wilderness savvy, they sought to get out of the woods instead of using them for cover. Going right toward what they knew, the town with its concrete and traffic lights, going right into the arms of the law.

They should have headed for Wilmington, lost themselves in the swamps, the silent dark pocosin, then faded into the wide anonymity of the Atlantic seaboard.

After the little killers had vacated, a group of Mormons moved in just for the weekend. A collection of angelic blond girls, all well-formed in face and limb, no spot or blemish, their teeth like alabaster, and their eyes like those of old-fashioned dolls, wide-open and blue as glass, fringed with dark lashes.

No Coca-Colas, no iced tea, no chocolate for these children. No stimulant of any kind. They were beloved of the Lord Jesus, waited for His imminent return, and came to borrow my cake pans early Saturday morning to bake a birthday cake for their leader.

A bevy of blonds decorated my doorsteps, maybe thirteen years old at the most, perfect suntans, crisp white shorts and halter tops embroidered with navy blue anchors, they clamored for my cake pans and exclaimed how they'd make such a wonderful cake, frost it in pink and light circles of pink candles around the top.

And they did, I supposed, for the pans were returned late the same day, washed and polished, more gleaming than they were before. And as I put them away, I noticed, close along one rim, tucked nearly inside the lip of the pan, a tiny swastika etched into the aluminum.

I pulled the cake pan closer and stared. I got the big magnifying glass and stared again. A perfect little swastika. Did they? Surely, they did not? Those little blond Mormons bubbling in good health and pink birthdays.

But the swastika wasn't on the cake pan before. At least, I didn't think it was. Maybe an accident, the scraping of a metal spatula, the shove of a blade to loosen the cooling cake—and the little twisted cross appeared. I put the pans away, let them clatter against the bundt pan, the cookie sheets in the utensil drawer under the oven.

The little blonds left the camp clean as a pin, clean as a whistle, spotless, stainless, snow-white, spic and span. Only clichés could describe it. Not one drop of hamburger blood on the butcher's block. Not one wilted lettuce leaf in the cooler. You'd never know they had been there.

Clyde approved. That's the way I like my camp left, cleaned up good, treated with respect. And he went on to tell how they were washing dishes in the mess hall and one little blond person told another to wash off the bottom of the Lemon Joy bottle.

I thought a minute. Don't you think that's kind of creepy?

He hugged me, looked around, teasing, It might be in this kitchen.

My dishes stacked up along the counter, soap bubbles winking and bursting. But they were absolutely clean, the Blue Willow gleaming. Sweet smells of oregano and bubbling tomato filled the kitchen. And my bottle of Lemon Joy sat in a sticky puddle of normal pungent ooze.

Toward the end of the summer, one of the cats, an offspring of old Thomas and Tar Baby, got zapped by lightning. A peculiar-looking cat with his dirty-white front part and his back part striped gray, Tigger's hind legs also stuck up too high. And he had big suspicious eyes. Never friendly or companionable, Tigger skulked around the house, peered at people from the lobelia bush, and never once came to be stroked. I didn't think Tigger even purred.

But the children had named him Tigger after the tiger in the Pooh stories, and they thought he was okay. They forgave him his personality and peevish ways.

They smelled something rotten, something outside the house, yet seeming to percolate from within it, too. Finally, Clyde located it behind the baffle-door that led under the house. As soon as he unlatched the door, the smell rushed out like an explosion. And spread-eagled on a piece of plumbing, an old iron pipe, was poor young Tigger, dead as dead could be.

Clyde concluded he was probably skulking under the house, sitting on the iron pipe to preen himself, when a thunderstorm came up and lightning struck.

—What a way to go, said Clyde.

Clyde had been struck by lightning himself, as a child taking a bath in an old ball-and-claw tub one summer. A storm blew up, and when Clyde got out, holding on to the iron shower pipe, *zap!* He said it knocked him down and addled his brain a moment. Then he was okay.

So Clyde sympathized with the cat. And as he dragged Tigger out to bury him in the woods, I noticed the cat's eyes were still big and suspicious. Melissa and Kirk stuck a twig cross over his grave. Tigger was not much missed.

But those big suspicious eyes. They showed up again in a few weeks. The camp filled with lively black children gathered to celebrate black tribal culture, African Methodist Episcopal Zion groups from Fayetteville and Tabor City. I liked to roll that off my tongue, *African Methodist Episcopal Zion.* Why couldn't white churches flaunt such poetry?

The children jumped into camping with great spirit. They played and swam, sang and ate and prayed, went on nature hikes, and modeled elaborate clay masks in the hot sun.

Melissa and Kirk and I on daily rambles often saw them grouped around bright plastic pails of water and kaolin, the sun glinting off their skin as they plunged their fists into the wet clay and squeezed and pressed and shaped huge faces. Ancestral faces, lips plumped to stylized pouts, flaring nostrils, and big round eye holes, as big as the cat Tigger's, and just as unfriendly.

After the groups went back to Fayetteville and Tabor City, Melissa and Kirk found some of their masks abandoned in the camp. They lugged the big heavy things back to the yard. Melissa got her water colors and painted cheeks and lips, adding mascara around the staring eye holes. Kirk pressed colored beads into his mask, adorning ear lobes and nostrils. I wish I had a bone, he said, I'd stick a bone through the nose.

The children treasured the masks. Seemed to feel they were powerful things, like relics or lucky charms. They believed in them. And also believed they had to stay outside in the yard to remain magic. I thought they might bring the masks inside, hang them in their rooms. But they said, no, the clay faces had to stay outside in the yard. They had more power outside.

But the unfired clay wouldn't keep. It melted with the first hard autumn rain. And any clay left after the rain turned chalky and flaked as it aged.

The children mourned the dying away of those masks as they had never mourned the cat Tigger.

I watched the melting clay in the rain, the flaking ear lobes and nostrils in the sun, and thought about the old parables in the Bible, the stories of potters and their clay. I thought of mud and loam and the vulnerable flesh of my two children, and the relentless melting away of all that Clyde and I both loved.

14
Leap Year

KATHLEEN TERRY WAS A FRIEND who came sometimes to sail on Singletary. The sailboat belonged to other friends of hers and they had christened it *Heather* for their young daughter. Watching that boat slide through the water, *Heather* glistening on its bow, I had the feeling I was watching myself under sail, feeling the heave, the dip into the wind, the shivers and tugs, the cold slap of the waves.

My daddy always declared he named me Heather to go with the Scottish surname Ross. But I think probably both he and my mother dragged it up from that 40s movie star called Heather Angel, a big-eyed girl given to heavy costume jewelry and coyly plucked brows, usually in movies with Randolph Scott or Cornel Wilde, all fleeing from Mohican Indians.

I wondered why Kathleen's friends with the sailboat named their daughter Heather. It didn't matter.

The children sailed with Kathleen. Clyde and I waited for them on the pier. They emerged silent as shadows at the mouth of the canal and advanced steadily across the lake to us, making no unnecessary noise, just the sounds of the wind and water working together. As they neared, we heard the creak of rope and sail, good sounds, like the clearest definition of honest labor.

Kirk and Melissa sat still, holding on and squinting their eyes against the glare, Kathleen like a captain behind them, her skillful hands managing everything, big smiles flushing her lips.

At certain rare times, Kathleen told us, when the wind and water are pulling exactly right and the tensions of sail and line are balanced, the boat gives a little tremor all over. You felt it, she said, through the bottom of the boat, up through your bare feet and legs, up through your body and out the top of your head. And you've had one of those moments you wait for all your life. Furthermore, said Kathleen, you never know you've been waiting for such a moment until it's over, slipped right on through you.

Those quiet afternoons on the lake, Kathleen held the rope and *Heather* turned straight with the wind, cutting open the bright cola water. Her maneuvers were crisp. The children enthralled. A scene to make you believe in good things.

We all believed in Kathleen Terry, her long curling hair, her husky call at the door, Hey, just me. If we had inclined to be reclusive, tried to resist Kathleen, she would have won the Millers anyway. Not a forceful woman, but a very cheerfully determined one. If the sounds of *Heather's* ropes and sails in the wind signified honest labor, then the sounds of Kathleen's warm speech and the resilience of her handshake signified friendship. She was a woman who coped. An intellectual and an artist, somebody who survived perils.

She taught a year at Whiteville High School before joining the faculty of Southeastern Community College in 1969 as a tutor-counselor in English. And that was how I met her, for by this time I'd started teaching there, too. She showed me her poems, and she bought my books. She chugged around Columbus County in a faded red Beetle, her dog Chap sitting up beside her. Kathleen wore wide leather watch-bands, her watches broad as compasses. She played the guitar, and shared the harsh rich music of Janis Joplin with us in the woods. Later she sold the red Beetle and got a motorcycle.

The motorcycle introduced her to a new world of perils. Her easy laughter had always won the world before. But you cannot laugh away a man in a pick-up truck driving straight at you on your motorcycle. A man who leans out to swing at you with a 2x4.

—First they think I'm a long-haired boy, she said, and that makes them mad. Then they see I'm a girl, and that makes them even madder. They just go crazy.

But Kathleen kept on riding the motorcycle. She gloried in the night wind on her face, the smell of honeysuckle and corn fields, the alternating patches of warm, then cool air along the road.

—You wouldn't think it, she said, the wonderful smells you pick up out there.

So, because she didn't worry, we didn't worry. Kathleen Terry could take care of herself. She made the fifty-five mile run from Whiteville to Singletary Lake Group Camp and back again okay. Just as easily as I did in the lumbering VW bus, Wolfgang.

But sometimes I couldn't help wanting to trade the bus for the motorcycle, go roaring off like Kathleen, my long hair flying like a crazy banner in the night.

I couldn't help thinking what it would be like to just go fearlessly into the world as she did, no children, no husband, no Crusoe. Just the woman and the wild machine. I was envious.

Kathleen also made pictures and then developed them herself, printed them up on glossy stock. I sent mine off to Jack Rabbit in

Kirk with the Christmas candle

Spartanburg, South Carolina. Kathleen's being able to bring her images straight out of the air and the hypo solution onto paper seemed far better. She made pictures of us and the best were of Melissa shadowed in mystical lamplight. Kirk lighting his home-made Christmas candle. And Clyde in profile, portraits of Melissa and Kirk a bit blurred on the dark wall behind.

I persuaded Kathleen her poems were good enough to earn her a Master of Fine Arts degree. Kathleen got accepted at Greensboro, and before she left, brought us one of Chap's pups. Black with tan markings over both eyes and a fuzzy, arched, rooster tail, Wilbur was the children's joy. And the old dog Poochie's immense hatred. Poochie aged one hundred years the day we got Wilbur. He quit sporting about in the leaves, quit retrieving pine cones. He even quit going on walks with us. Every time Wilbur came near, wagging his rooster tail, Poochie snapped. A sharp squeal, a whimper, and the children announced, Poochie bit Wilbur again! and ran out to chastise the old dog. After a while, Wilbur learned which side of the yard to stay on.

We missed Kathleen and the pleasant sailing afternoons. She wrote short newsy letters from Greensboro, and when I went up there on February 29, 1972, Leap Year Day, to teach several poetry-in-schools sessions at local high schools, Kathleen came over to visit me at the Hilton. It was warm for February, daffodils popping up, making the place smell fresh and yellow. My room on the sixth floor had a full view of the dirty noisy city. Kathleen and I ordered coffee and doughnuts from room service and when it came, spread across the lavish Hilton beds to feast and talk.

We talked late, the lights coming on over Greensboro and the traffic screeching. Kathleen's strong face looked the same, her hair still healthy and curly and flying in all directions. But Kathleen was different, nervous, looking over her shoulder, going to the window, testing the lock on the door. She had taken on a darker depth.

I asked her what she kept looking at, what she thought was out there.

She smiled, I don't know.

Then Kathleen told me how she got attacked on her paper route right beside the UNC-G golf course, in plain view of the residents, most of them her own clients. She delivered the evening paper on a bicycle and was pedaling across a small parking lot when a man jumped from behind a car and started following her. Kathleen got off the bike and faced him.

—I did the worst thing I could've done, she said, I threw the bike at him and that put him on the defensive.

He came at her with both hands, chased her, and caught her by the long curly hair, wrestled her to the ground, choking and hitting her in her face.

—He kept saying, You bitch! And I kept saying, You bastard!

He put a gun to her head. This here's a gun, you bitch. Do you believe me, bitch? I'll blow your head off, you don't come on. You hear, bitch.

He pushed Kathleen toward a car at the curb. That, she declared, was when she pulled together all the strength and guts she had, broke free, and ran to the nearest house. She beat and kicked until two old ladies opened it and let her inside.

They'd been watching the whole thing, they told her.

Only later, Kathleen said, she realized she had been struggling with a black man. It's funny, but we never once said, You black nigger or You white cunt. We just said, You bastard and You bitch.

Our coffee mugs clinked in the stuffy sweet air of the Hilton room. Kathleen broke apart a big glazed doughnut, as rich and yellow as the Leap Year daffodils outside, and crumbled it on her saucer. People passed down the corridor arguing.

In the Greensboro police station, two white detectives in raincoats told Kathleen, Yah, you're lucky. You're still alive because you're a mature woman and you used your common sense. Yah, you're damn lucky.

—Shit, said Kathleen to me, I'm still alive because I was scared and I got loose and those two old ladies finally decided to open the damn door.

After Kathleen left, I looked out the sixth-floor window a long time. The lights of Greensboro glittered and stayed busy. Still warm as spring out there, those daffodils flourishing in people's yards. Leap Year, a year of 366 days, one extra February day and night right there in plain Greensboro and all over the world, making up for time lost those other four years of 365 and one-fourth days.

I put a call through to my sleeping family in Bladen County and let it ring awhile. Nobody would answer, it was too deep into the night, already March 1, Clyde snoring, the two children sprawled in their beds, Poochie on one side of the white sandy yard, Wilbur on the other. I knew this before I'd finished dialing. But I listened to the phone ring and pictured how it was there, the sleeping house, the roof, the chimney, the whorled pine panels, and the phone ringing in a corner, and the dark woods crowding every side. It made me feel better, a long link back to where I belonged. To where I always wanted to stay.

Clyde and I never saw Kathleen again. A few phone calls. The letters stopped. We heard she had gone to Long Island to work in a project to get women off the streets. We heard she was in jail. Then heard nothing.

Oddly enough, the pup Wilbur got hit by a motorcycle that roared down the highway just beyond the park gate. Kirk, playing in a patch of trees between the park shops and the highway, heard the whole thing. First the motorcycle's roar and squall, then Wilbur's high yelp, then nothing. He hurried to the scene, knowing exactly what he would find, and suffered more than anybody, bursting into the kitchen, Wilbur's dead! and then crying worse when I at first didn't believe him.

—You know, he sobbed, it was worse hearing it than seeing it. I just knew, Mama, I just knew.

Melissa wrote a eulogy, and Clyde buried poor little Wilbur in the sand beside of Kelly Star Route. When we all got back to the house, old Poochie was rejuvenated, cavorting through the leaves, bright-eyed and utterly delighted, a new dog. He snarled at pine cones, throwing them up and chasing them, celebrating to see us again, his own family, rivaled no longer by a rooster-tailed pup. Nobody blamed him. Nobody ever blames a poor old dog.

Whatever other families might live in that dark-paneled park house after we Millers might leave, I wished them adventure and curiosity. The glossy cola-colored lake, without fail, would flash and ripple in both summer and winter. And I, wherever I might be, would wonder what ghosts played in the woods around it, what dogs and cats, two children, a man and a woman. What phantom sailboats might cut the surface of Singletary Lake, a tremor blossoming from keel to topsail. I wondered if anyone would guess at the mystery of Crusoe's Island.

At the excitement of Kathleen on that sailboat and astride that motorcycle. At the remarkable envy I felt, her long wild hair and her presence.

15

Uncommonly Deep Snow

ONE NIGHT SNOW STARTED FALLING unexpectedly and covered the ground before Clyde and I noticed. We had our feet up in front of a big cheerful fire, so at first he scoffed when I wanted to go outside in the snow. But he gave in.

We dragged the sled from the park garage and had been frolicking all over the white yard when we happened to look up and see Melissa watching. Our carrying-on had waked her, and she sat nose to the glass, a patch of breath clouding around her face.

Clyde said, Let's go get Melissa. And so we burst inside, bundled her in blankets, not bothering to dress her properly, and then pulled her around in the dark woods, each tree outlined by the falling snow. Melissa sat on the sled, blinking back the flakes. We must have seemed like two Big Presences to her, two gods at play in the middle of a snowfall. She never said a thing, just looked and grinned and loved it.

When Kirk found this out in the morning, he was annoyed. He said he wished Clyde and I'd waked him up, too. He said he would have stayed out all night in the snow. But he got us all back. While Clyde and I enjoyed a mug of coffee over in the park office, Kirk shed his clothes and embarked on his snow adventure, jumping naked into a snow bank and rolling around making snow angels, and then running all the way around the house, his butt, Melissa later said, red as fire.

We never knew a thing about that nude frolic in the snow until after a few days, Melissa prompted Kirk, Why don't you take off all your clothes and go jump in the snow naked again?

He made a funny face. It's not as much fun as I thought it was going to be, he said. I thought it was going to be all soft and fluffy. It made my feet hurt.

—When'd you do that? I asked, Why'd you do that?

I blinked at him. The lazy snow drifted around the house, and I envisioned my son dashing madly through the wilderness, the snow shocking his feet, his skin raising goose bumps, and the dark glossy hair of his head crackling with electricity.

He grinned, You and Daddy didn't know a thing about it.

Kirk was a good person to frolic in the snow with. The kind of boy to see a moonbow in the middle of the winter, that endless circle of thin light ladled down upon us from the cold white moon. The kind of boy to call me to look at it with him, both of us washed in the widening circle of moonlight reflected off deep snow.

The deepest snow blew into the park one January from the Atlantic Ocean fifty miles away. It caught everybody unprepared. Schools closed for weeks. Pregnant women had to be helicoptered to the hospital. In the middle of the swirling flakes, we heard thunder, and then lightning knocked out our central heat. But we didn't lose the lights or the water heater. So we were able to cook and have steaming hot baths.

We closed up the house, curtained all the icy windows. Clyde kept a big fire going on the hearth, and we slept around it at night in blankets, feet to hot water bottles. So long as we stuck to the hearth, we were cozy. Anytime we moved to the kitchen or the bathroom, we got a bitter chill.

The children loved all this. And Clyde and I did, too, after a fashion. We ate cozy suppers around the fire, enjoying each other's company, visiting in ways that we'd neglected before the central heat died. Nobody even thought about looking at television.

Early in the morning, Melissa and Kirk brought me the freshest, most choice snow in big plastic bowls and I made snow cream, mixing the clean white snow with a thin vanilla and egg custard. Everybody spooned it up heartily, even Clyde who usually ignored sweets. It tasted of such an exotic flavoring, a strong harmony of wild snow and vanilla and egg, easing over the tongue, slipping down the throat. Our teeth tingled.

—You're sure nothing peed in this snow? Clyde asked the children.

They shrieked, *No!* Nothing peed in this snow!

The snow brought clean crisp smells suffused with wood smoke and wet woolies, smells to put a sharp edge on things, and wake you up. We trudged out those cold nights, following Indian-style in a narrow white trench, to gaze at the stars. Such a peculiar luminosity reflecting off both snow and sky, both so pearly and smooth, you felt you might be able to reach out and stroke the whole world, model it into shapes.

The dog Poochie floundered in drifts up to his belly and sneezed. The black cats burrowed close to the house, just past the drip line, and stayed there, the snow actually over their heads, thir-

Kirk and Melissa, Big Snow, 1973

teen inches deep. They were full of static electricity and brushed around the children's legs, purring.

Drifts were reported down to the water's edge at Wrightsville and Carolina Beach and Kure. Each day toward noon, as the temperature warmed just a fraction, ice broke off the Channel 6 tower that stood in a cleared field to the left of the park entrance. The ice gave a loud crack and cascaded down in glittering shards. The cables showed brilliant white for a moment against the sky, then flashed black and wet. The next morning, when we went out to look for the mail, the cables would be white and heavy again.

But it was weeks before the mail passed again. Kelly Star Route, its shoulders muted under snow, stretched toward White Lake, the big pines shrouded like ghosts.

Singletary Lake froze solid from the shore out beyond the end of the long pier, at least thirty feet, snow hanging in the Spanish moss thick as cotton candy. The children slid on the ice, then explored the hard-frozen swamps. They called us to examine the strange hard scummy ice formed near the shore, capturing cypress needles and feathers and cones like some kind of disturbing Lucite witch's ball.

—Looks nasty, Melissa said.

I agreed. Nasty, but curious. She poked it with a long stick.

The dog could walk farther out on the ice than the children, padding carefully, his toenails making a delicate scratch on the thin rime. He stayed way out on the frozen lake, orbiting them like a satellite, and literally walking on water.

We spotted a bobcat. Its silky gray fur showed greenish-yellow spots, and its face, more cat-looking, somehow, than Thomas or Tar Baby, brushed out either side with big white mutton chops.

The bobcat watched us awhile, calm, inquisitive. Kirk shivered and held a glove to his mouth.

—A big old bobcat, he said, chewing a finger of the glove.

The bobcat turned then and, like a shadow, blended into the pond bay along the trail and vanished. There, whispered Kirk. A big old bobcat looking at us. And he shivered again, though wrapped in his woolly cap and heavy jacket, jeans stuffed deep inside black cowboy boots.

We surprised a flock of ducks at the spillway. They took to the air, and we counted at least thirty flapping and quacking over the lake. Then back at the house, Clyde set up the barbecue grill in the snow and we feasted on hot dogs with the children. Nothing so tantalizing as a burned weenie with mustard and onions when you're hungry from tramping the deep snow.

One morning Melissa made a Snow Madonna. The round white child looked up at his mother with a sweet dopey contour to her face. And she cradled him in cold white arms festooned in gray moss. Kirk made a Snow Shepherd to guard mother and child, and jammed Clyde's snake-killing hoe under his white arm for a crosier.

That Adoration in the Snow stuck around a long time. Even after the snow began to melt and the children finally went back to school, those lumps of solid white persisted. I noticed them especially at night if I stepped outside for a fresh breath. At the edge of the woods, they waited cold and hard against the black trees and even blacker sky, the ice crystals sparkling in the park security light. The woman's face still sweet and dopey, the child like a white circle, and the shepherd keeping watch with his hoe. A stubborn group, they clung to their place in the yard.

After a while, though, our numb fingers and feet got to be tiresome, along with woolly caps and wet gloves and boots, the shivering and the blinding whiteness. For days we'd been cut off. No telephone. No easy transportation into Elizabethtown possible because the road hadn't yet been cleared. One morning, the children looked out to see Ivory McCoy's little boys standing in the snow, their feet wrapped up in plastic bread wrappers.

—Hey! they hollered, You wants to play!

Kirk rushed right out and played with them all morning, dragging the sled around, helping them push each other on it as well as on big shiny garbage can lids. Melissa stayed inside drawing cartoons until she had a whole book. Then she took it out and made everybody look at it, standing in a circle.

They were the only people we saw until the furnace man plowed through the snow in his big purple car with tail fins and chains. He didn't have a truck, and he actually came out on a Sunday afternoon. The snow flew up on either side of him like the wake of a ship. Within minutes, the central heat clicked back on

Kirk, Singletary Lake pier, 1973

and we got toasty warm, the gloves and the boots drying out, our skins rosy, and our tempers improved.

He brought fire to us in the snowy wilderness, a genuine gift-giver. All because we were his regular customers, and he had us on his mind and made the fifty-mile round trip out just to check.

—Didn't want y'all freezing to death and nobody not knowing about it, he drawled, throwing tools back in the big car. It was one of those customized things, all the factory chrome removed, and the body waxed to a metallic purple. Except for huge black brogans, he wore only street clothes, no cap or gloves. And he had a long glittering watch chain looping from his left pocket way down almost to his knee. He smiled with a jaw packed full of tobacco.

Clyde watched him maneuver the purple car around and cruise back through the snow. Said, Well, you never know how Jesus might look when he comes again.

I thought, Yes, with a chaw and purple tailfins. And a long long watch chain.

Clyde and I'd thought of ourselves as healthy and self-sufficient, able to live out there in the woods. We didn't need a lot of things. But when we heard that noisy furnace click on and felt the fan start pushing warm air around the cold house, we almost got drunk, the warmth and the relief were so intoxicating.

In Wallace Stevens's poem, "The World as Meditation," Penelope wakes and feels the morning sun move toward her like the approaching, long-absent Ulysses. She feels comforted, and falls in love with him all over again. She and her husband are:

> *Two in a deep-founded sheltering,*
> *Friend and dear friend.*

Clyde and I read to each other in bed, and by the fire, throughout the long snow, the cold woods and the pocosin spreading beyond the house. I read those lines from the poem to Clyde and he learned them, said, That's the way we are. Two, friend and dear friend.

The lines became a motto. And whenever I was away from Crusoe, or he was away, we wrote to each other, "Friend and dear friend," sometimes, "Playmate, lover, dear, dear friend."

We were two in a deep-founded sheltering, talking to each other every day in natural true verbs, teaching each other survival. If the woods were wild outside, the house of dark pine panels was deep-founded. All parts of that life were unusual and strong. No false comforts, no hypocrisies. Not a life of ease, but a good life. You either made it yours, or you didn't.

And he ministered to me, to the things I tried to do, the stories I made. I came home from teaching and there set up on the dining table was a brand-new Smith-Corona. He'd gone to Lumberton, gotten rid of the old Royal at some office equipment place, and come back with this surprise for me.

I loved it, the surprise of it, the charm of it.

—That's your Merry Un-Birthday present, he said.

The very merry un-birthday present from Alice's mad tea party, from this quiet and self-contained man who brought me here and showed me things I'd never thought of.

And later, after more books got written on that Smith-Corona, after more teaching, I came home to another surprise. He had searched for months until he found, somewhere in a coastal Carolina used school-equipment warehouse, the biggest desk I'd ever seen. Somehow he'd gotten it back to Singletary, into the shops, and refinished it until it shone with all the luster of honey and had the feel of satin. An amazing desk, a schoolteacher's, with slide panels and secret drawers, a huge wide surface, slick as glass, and a presence solid as Gibraltar.

Rayvon helped him move it into the house and set it up in the back bay, what once was the nursery, now my writing place. It sat there right by the windows, right where Kirk's crib once stood.

I fell in love all over.

Rayvon wiped his face, said, That'airs the slickest piece of big old furnytoor I ever seen in my whole life! He accented the last part, my *'ollafe!*

I caressed the desk. I kissed it. I opened the Smith-Corona, sat down and gazed out the windows at the rows and rows of pines blowing with Spanish moss. I felt good. I wanted to run out and kiss the whole world. *Th'olworl!*

I sat there and gazed at sun and rain, at spring and winter, and I wrote what I could. And promised to imagine all the rest. This:

In the woods, morning snow always fell in a persistent mist with birds calling and squirrels quarreling in the big trees around the house. The children went out with their sled, booted and muffled and disappeared, laughing, into the snow. Then the man, in a black regulation parka and thick gloves, went out, too. He looked like a beast man, an Eskimo. The snow kept on falling.

And as one bird called to another, the woman herself went to the door and let the snow fall in her face. She smiled up into its thousands of little cold hands. The flakes patted her face, sealed her eyelashes. Bigger flakes began to fall, and she thought, Well, if I had the persistence of the snow, if I could make friends with the snow and the woods, if I figured out how it all worked . . .

And then this woman, who is me, wrote it in a book. She knew it was one of those moments you wait for all your life. And only after it happens, do you realize you have been waiting.

16

The Palmer Christian

Bladen Lakes State Forest let us dump trash in a pit deep in the sand and turkey oaks off Kelly Star Route. Clyde and Newbold Pait, the superintendent of Jones Lake State Park, both on the site late that same winter, noticed a gigantic plant growing near the rim of the pit. Tall as a man, it spread large over the smaller turkey oaks.

Newbold said, Look at that old palmer Christian.

Clyde was amazed so large a plant could still be hanging on in the bitter cold. Newbold said, No, couldn't nothing kill that old palmer Christian.

Clyde, still amazed, not only by the showy plant, but also by its provocative name, palmer Christian, took me to see it. We glided along in the park pickup, grinding the soft, pine-needled sand. As soon as I got out of the truck, I spotted it.

The palmer Christian, though shriveled from the cold, rustled large palm-like leaves. I blinked at its thick canes and clusters of burrs with seeds tight inside, touched them, and shivered. Everything around us loomed gray and still. Some red leaves rattled on the turkey oaks, but most of the trees were bare as bones, standing around like frozen bouquets. The whole place appeared to be waiting for something with an apprehensive patience the deep woods have.

I focused the Exakta on the palmer Christian and shot. The picture later came out grainy black and white, as cold as the winter afternoon. Every time I looked at it, I touched a finger lightly to the burrs clustered at the leaves. And remembered how hard I tried to pull up a few of the palmer Christian shoots, but they were too tough for me. Clyde broke off some branches with burrs, and I rode back with them in my lap like a bride.

I held my hand to one of the leaves. Star-shaped, the dark green lobes like the fingers of a human hand, it also looked like a palm branch. Why did they call it the palmer Christian? Why was it in a garbage pit in Bladen County, defying the coldest season of the year?

Newbold Pait said his mother used to parch the leaves in her oven and then put them under the children's beds to break a fever. She steeped the dry leaves in a teacup of hot water and got the children to inhale the fumes when they had stomach aches.

—She used that stuff a lot in the spring, or the first of the summer when the grapes got ripe, and we ate us too many, he said. That old palmer Christian stunk so bad, we'd forget we was sick.

He remembered his mother planting the palmer Christian on purpose in the yard. Won't no weed to her, and she always called it that old palmer Christian.

Newbold spread out his hand. Well, it sorta looks like your hand.

But nothing about the way the plant looked suggested to him what it suggested to me: palm branches, Christ's triumphal entry into Jerusalem, the healing powers of Christ, Christ's hand nailed to the cross.

Newbold remembered other things. You get the chicken pox, he shook a finger, you can do two things: get in the chicken lot and let 'em fly over your head. Or take a little of that tea from that old palmer Christian. Take it in the late afternoon. Otherwise, he cautioned, it ain't no good.

That spring, I got a manual on exotic plants from the library, and soon found the palmer Christian was the red castor bean plant, bold and striking, often reaching forty feet. The giant leaves divided into five or eleven lobes, one to three feet across, bronzy and dark red, coloring more deeply as they aged. The seeds in the burrs, mottled and bean-like, were so poisonous two could kill a young child.

I shook my head and shivered, smoothing the sepia photograph of the castor bean. I'd been carrying a branch of the palmer Christian around in the back of the car for weeks. Just two of its seeds could have killed either or both my children. I kept reading. Considered a tropical evergreen, the castor bean was quite hardy, able to endure sudden changes in temperature, warm days and bitter cold nights, and easily tolerated neglect.

No wonder it flourished by the sand pit in the late winter, still clinging to life and leaves when all the other trees had gone dormant. Showy and useful, beautiful and deadly. A hundred varieties.

This was a quite natural plant to be growing in the middle of the woods, unaware of its many talents, growing alone and tenacious. Probably dropped there by a bird. Or thrown away in some yard clippings.

These were easy summations, but they lacked charm, had none of Newbold Pait's human storytelling touches, the stomach aches and the chicken pox. I wrote it all up and published a little article in the *North Carolina Folklore Journal*. Most of all, I asked in the article, why was this thing called the palmer Christian?

I got some mail, a letter and a postcard from people who read my article. They told me more things about the castor bean, stories like Newbold's.

—That's the meanest plant in the whole state of North Carolina, declared the postcard. You can't hardly kill it.

A package of castor bean seeds came folded inside the letter. The lady told me to plant them in a part of the yard where nothing else grew. They'll take, she said, just like a chinaberry tree. You'll get your money's worth.

But nobody said anything about the folk name, palmer Christian.

I started to put the seeds out next to the yucca, near a dry clump of azaleas I'd failed to raise. The dog frolicked in the sand, nosing up a big pine cone and barking. The children stayed busy on the swings. There seemed nothing deadly or mysterious in the yard, no hand of Christ, no palm branches. But what if the castor bean thrived in this place, shot up to a bushy, rustling forty feet? What if it dropped its poisonous seeds and the children ate them, the dog, the two black cats?

I would warn them. I would tell them this was poison and don't touch it.

But what if they did it anyway?

I put the spading fork away and decided to forget it.

A few weeks later, another postcard. This woman told me her daddy always planted castor beans deliberately around his yard to deter moles.

—Moles hate a castor bean, she said. You get a mole in your yard, plant a castor bean.

She'd never heard of the palmer Christian.

I photographed many other impressive plants at Crusoe. Pipeworts and hooded pitcher plants, the sticky sundews, bird's-foot violets, ipecac, and the famous Venus fly-trap, noted by William Bartram in his early explorations of the Carolina bay lakes, particularly Green Swamp in Columbus County, due south of them.

I got out on the shoulders of Kelly Star Route in the middle of July, heat boiling off the asphalt, and took pictures of things I thought might not last the summer. Or the Department of Transportation mowing crews. Woolly mullein five feet tall flowered in fragrant patches, the blossoms like yellow moths. Blue lupine, pink cowpeas, and pokeweed, the ripe berries glistening dark purple. I took pokeberries back and showed the children how to make ink.

—Don't eat any, though, I warned, don't even lick the tip of your pen. Or your fingers. Or anything. It's poison.

—Poison, pronounced Melissa as solemnly as she'd once pronounced *Claws*, mimicking my tone about the geoasters.

Clyde told a story about some tenants, the Burrises, who farmed his daddy's land when he was a child back in the Piedmont. A whole family of girls, he loved to go play with them, especially Canty Bell, who was his age, about five.

We watched Melissa sketch a purple horse running, its tail spread in the wind. Kirk printed his name in big letters, then added a clown face. They painted on sheets of newsprint, and the wild ink spread quickly, blurred the horse, the clown, the name.

—One time, Clyde said, the Burrises were all out in the yard eating pokeberries right off the bushes.

—That's poison, Kirk pointed his pen at the saucer of berry juice. 'Cause Mama said.

Clyde nodded. But they acted like it was so good and they wanted me to eat some, too, so I did.

Clyde rubbed his stomach. Boy, I got so sick. I just about puked myself to death.

Clyde said he was dumb to eat the pokeberries. But the Burrises didn't get sick, and Canty Bell was just shoveling them in her mouth.

I thought about those little girls, all blond heads and sunburned faces, shoveling pokeberries in their purple mouths. Then of Clyde, knowing better and doing it anyway.

—Why didn't they get sick?

—I don't know. They ate everything. Just used to it, I guess.

Maybe the berries weren't as poisonous as I thought. Maybe it was just the leaves and roots. Grandmother Martha Anna Smith gathered poke salad in the spring, the tender new shoots, and boiled them with lots of pork, changing the water three times.

—If you don't change the water three times, Grandmother Martha Anna said, they'll kill you.

She thought nothing better for a spring tonic than poke salad. She dipped Railroad Mills snuff until her eighties, outliving by forty years my grandfather who blew himself to pieces with a shotgun.

I thought what curious mixtures my children must be.

I thought what curious delights the world brings.

So many years ago, now, we came to Singletary Lake Group Camp at Christmas. Baby Melissa and I had picked some geoasters. And now here was Melissa a proper young lady, with a brother called Kirk Miller.

I can't believe it. Such good luck.

Clyde had my best shots mounted as colored slides and used them in his occasional nature talks that the park service referred to as

Kirk and Melissa examine Spanish moss on a turkey oak

general interpretative education. I hoped all the plants I found at Crusoe's Island had strong curative powers, enough to incite passion, drive out demons, make purple ink, and boil up a spring tonic. I never doubted such possibilities. Anything could be found in the woods. You could cure yourself, if you wanted, just by sitting in the middle of the woods on a sunny day.

Kirk could. He woke in the morning with a raging fever, headache, queasy stomach. At noon, after tossing around in bed, he got up to sit in the yard. Lie down flat down on the sand and stretch himself full length in the sun and peer up into the blue bowl of a clear autumn day.

Then he said, Mama, rub my arms, rub my legs, rub out the sick.

I crouched beside Kirk, considering where his faith came from, and then without further question, I rubbed his arms and legs. Sometimes we stayed out together the whole afternoon, the dog and cats nosing us, squirrels scolding from the turkey oaks. Not a cloud in the sky. Kirk dozed. I read with a book in one hand, rubbing out Kirk's sick with the other.

We sat there until the school bus brought Melissa. She found us smelling like dry leaves and hot sun, smelling like Poochie and the cats, smelling like Crusoe's Island.

—Hey, what're y'all doing?

Kirk rolled over. Nothing.

And the next morning, he was well, devouring a stack of pancakes oozing maple syrup. The outside cured me, he always said. And Mama, too, rubbing out the sick.

That was a genuine laying-on of hands. I watched it happen more than once. I even tried it myself, getting Kirk or Melissa to rub out the headaches, the cricks in my neck, the tennis elbows. If I put myself into it, let the clear air and hot sun mix with the smell of drying leaves, or with the tang of spring buds. If I welcomed the generous laying-on of a child's hands. If I believed in the woods, then I healed.

Clyde was not so fortunate with his laying-on of hands, actually a tying-on of onion poultices. The worst thing happened, something he purely hated, and I did, too. A silly thing. And a thing of low medical importance. Hookworm. The parasite of the poor South. The malady of the region. It did not go with a place like Crusoe's Island. But he got it. We didn't know how. We bathed and showered, even when the water had been the color of strong tea. We had good teeth. We never went barefoot. The dogs and cats relieved themselves out in the woods. And neither of the children had ever suffered any kind of parasite.

Where did this pesky and evil hookworm originate?

We concluded maybe it came from Black Lake, an area that was being drained and reclaimed in an effort to get clear water of the kind enjoyed at White Lake. Since Black Lake was part of the North Carolina bay lakes, Clyde often made routine visits and checked on the progress of the water filtering process. Maybe the thing got on him there? We never, never knew. Most people wouldn't care where it came from. But we liked to run things down to their origin, if we could. Then we had a connection.

In any case, whatever its origin, the hookworm gave Clyde a terrible fit, itching and gnawing and migrating all over his foot, just one foot, and that was enough. You could see its migration, a little red thread traveling over the delicate skin of Clyde's instep, around his ankle, into the flesh of his sole.

The doctor gave him some pills. But the torment only increased. As if the thing got mad. So then Rayvon said to tie a poultice of onions around the foot, up to the ankle. I chopped a big white onion and dumped it into a plastic baggie and tied it around Clyde's ankle. The idea was the hookworm couldn't stand the smell. So would exit. So would smother in onion juice.

Even more torment. Clyde had to hobble around with the onions in the house, sleep with the baggie sticking out from under the cover at night. The onions fermented into a bubbling vibrant yellow. The smell came through the baggie. Everybody got up and left the room when Clyde came in. And the thing itched and itched.

We told Rayvon the poultice didn't work. He scratched his head, grinned, said, Wal, sometimes them things don't do no good. He stood there awhile just blinking and rubbing his overall buckles. Then he brightened, added, When I had the hookworm, I got so fed up, finally I just taken my pocketknife and cut the sonszeebitches out!

Clyde went back to the doctor and this time got the sonszeebitches frozen with dry ice. Sprayed right on the foot, as much as was safe to use. Carbon dioxide. It did the trick. The hookworm stopped traveling, no more little red thread, no more maddening itch.

It took Clyde a while to get over the whole idea, the disgusting image. Hookworm. Things invading his bloodstream, his lungs, his intestines. His unsuspecting foot.

The sonszeebitches.

17
The Candlewalk, the Watch

BUT MAYBE THOSE WERE BAPTIZINGS of pure love, of being tested in the wilderness. And maybe you'd never know anything better.

Other baptizings, though, took place in Singletary Lake. A popular place with charismatic groups. They always chose the coldest day in March to baptize each other.

Clyde made a show of paddling out in a boat with poles and rings. Drifted like a frog on a fiberglass lily pad, his regulation green straw hat pulled low on his head, sunglasses catching the hard sun. The children and I watched from a clump of juniper, just off the trail. We had a good view of the pier.

A brisk wind puckered the water as the candidates for baptism came down the trail and filed onto the pier. All girls and middle-aged women dressed in pajamas and bathrobes. We saw rosebud chenille go by, flannelette, crimson velour, one Cat Woman outfit. The preacher waited, waist deep, at the first dock rope, all the little orange floats bobbing behind him. He must have been freezing in that dark water.

Each candidate took off her shoes and climbed into the lake, and the preacher hollered something back at the people on the pier. Then lifted his arms to the sky and prayed, pinched the candidate's nose shut, ducked her under with a splash, and yanked her back.

Everybody applauded. The newly baptized person struggled to the pier and climbed up to get wrapped in towels and put her shoes on. All the while, Clyde watched from his fiberglass boat, prepared to save bodies.

An old-time baptizing. Like John baptizing Jesus in Jordan, the poor old preacher, teeth chattering, ducked each one under the living Singletary water, dark as Coca-Cola, and lifted her back to glory.

I admired the grit of those girls and women to go into the freezing March water. They had a true faith. And perhaps a true healing, a laying-on of hands as powerful and generous as Kirk's. A poultice more vibrant than Rayvon's.

Those humble people in their baptismal pajamas and towels used the lake for a good thing. They invested the dark water with a natural holiness. They stepped down into it, washed away their sins, then quietly departed, disturbing nothing.

But the professional Holy Rollers who rented the group camp for as long as two weeks always tried to take over the whole park, driving off other park users, preaching against and accusing and carrying on about anything that offended their fractious Christian sensibilities. They wouldn't let anybody bring babies around the camp. A crying baby jarred charismatic concentration. One old camp missionary, a veteran of many such summers, told me, Anytime a dang baby cries, every dang woman in here wants to go to it.

Imagine him saying *dang* baby, *dang* woman.

His name was Creech, and that always seemed exactly right to me. He wouldn't let boys and girls swim together, and they all had to wear bathrobes down to the water's edge. Mr. Creech wanted them to get right in and let the water cover them up so nobody would ogle their bodies.

He stuck up signs proclaiming *Singletary Lake Group Camp Bible Camp—Praise the Lord!* over the regular park informational signs. Clyde had to go around every summer and take these signs down. He tried to explain to Mr. Creech that the park belonged not to God, but to man.

The holy rollers got many phone calls in the middle of the night. Mysterious passings-away. Mysterious birthings. Clyde dressed and took these messages to them. They came back, scrubbing their eyes, to return the calls. Clyde accommodated their every need, if possible. He ran spiders and mild garter snakes out of their showers. He ordered special nonalcoholic vanilla flavorings for their desserts. But he refused to ban other park users from the general areas just to satisfy Mr. Creech.

So it was bound to happen, Armageddon, when some of the other people, cutting through the inner sanctum of *Singletary Lake Group Camp Bible Camp—Praise the Lord!*, casually lit up a cigarette. Insults were tossed. Somebody balled up a fist. And a skirmish broke out.

Mr. Creech and his flock crowded my doorstep shouting, Ma'am! We're trying to preach the Lord Jesus to these young people. And then somebody comes through smoking a dang cigarette. Maybe even drinking likker! Maybe even got somebody else's wife! Ma'am, you got to get your husband to stop this dang wickedness! Where's your dang husband!

I'd had a bad day. The ribbon jammed in the Smith-Corona. I got several rejections in the mail with arrogant notes attached. The children quarreled. And Clyde was gone to Raleigh on park business. He wouldn't be back until late.

I couldn't help it. I began crying great big tears the size of shiny snails. They slid down my face and dripped off my chin. Shut up! I yelled at Mr. Creech.

He shut up a moment, staring at me. Then he tried to take my hand. Ma'am, he asked, Do you know the Lord?

I slammed the screen door in his face and latched it. Dashed into the house and locked the front door. Mr. Creech and his people huddled there a moment longer, stupefied, then left.

When Clyde got back, he had to mediate this. He told the Holy Rollers to leave the other park users alone. He told the cigarette smokers to stay in their designated areas. He told me to have a sip of wine and calm down.

—I'm calm! Calm! I insisted.

The cigarette smokers wanted to apologize. Mr. Creech wanted to pray. I hated them all.

The next summer, in one of the hottest and driest Julys we ever had, Singletary Lake dried up to the end of the pier. I happened to ramble one afternoon with the children along the trail that followed the shore. It happened also to be when Mr. Creech had a gang of little boys out swimming. They splashed, free and unafraid, when a huge water snake slithered right through the middle of them, just trying to get on to what little water remained.

The little boys hollered, churned Singletary into suds as they panicked for the pier and then for the shore. And as we watched, expecting Mr. Creech to come call Clyde to kill that water snake, instead we heard him, declare, Listen to me. God A'mighty put that snake in this dang water before God A'mighty put you in it. Listen to me, that snake's minding his own dang bidness. So you just mind your own dang bidness.

Kirk, standing there in his favorite No. 55 football tee, his hair in long dark Beatle-bangs, said, That's smart. That makes sense. He liked Mr. Creech saying that. So I had to relent. I had to let

Melissa in the shallows of Singletary Lake

Mr. Creech mind his own dang business. And just mind my own dang business, too.

And even more baptizings occurred, genuine testings, trials by ordeal. These built the exotic folklore of the region. Newbold Pait told me stranger things connected to the palmer Christian. Things that stirred my spirit and curiosity. Built stronger layers onto my deepening respect for the place. And showed me my insignificant presence in it.

—They carry that old palmer Christian in church sometimes, he said, everybody carries one. But mostly they carry a candle for the candlewalk. Them old palmer Christians stink too bad.

—What's a candlewalk? I pressed.

—It's on Christmas Eve or on New Year's Eve, he said. Everybody knows you do a candlewalk then.

—But what is it?

Newbold laughed, a bit embarrassed. He was picking up a truckload of firewood for the campsites at Jones Lake. The crisp smell of the fresh-cut oak tingled my nose. Rayvon was helping load.

—I heard tell of them candlewalks, he said. It's a place out yonder on Highway 242 does them things.

Newbold agreed. Saints Delight, he said. Little bitty old place in the woods off the road.

Highway 242 lay in the general vicinity of Bladen Lakes State Forest, the northeast part of Bladen County. Shallow marshes, thick with turkey oaks and pines, many with Spanish moss, some with big clumps of mistletoe.

—But, I pressed again, tell me what it is, what's a candlewalk?

Newbold and Rayvon both hesitated, though continued to stack and load the cut wood. Wal, said Rayvon, I don't know too much about them things. But they is religious things. They is real religious things.

—It's just a thing you do most of the time on New Year's Eve, said Newbold. The women come inside the church with a candle where the men is already. And then you walk around the church singing and praising God for the new year. He stopped, lit a cigarette. This is at midnight. When the new year comes.

He drew on the cigarette a moment. Oh, he said, I forgot. All the women are dressed up in white, or sometimes a white sheet. It's a nice thing, you know. He threw down the cigarette, ground it underfoot.

—Wal, said Rayvon, I heard tell couldn't no white people go to them things. He wiped his face, grinned at Newbold. That's what they tell me.

—No, Newbold grinned back. That ain't the way. It depends on the people, on the congregation. If you a white person and you a believer, then sometimes you can come on. But one thing for sure, can't no nonbelievers come.

By this time the truck was loaded and Newbold drove off, waving back at me and Rayvon Kinlaw.

Rayvon watched the green truck pass down the park road and pick up speed on Kelly Star Route. Wal, he said, you know what I heard tell?

And before I could say a word, he launched into his spectacular version of what happened in a candlewalk in Saints Delight out somewhere close to Highway 242.

—Them women and all them girls go way out in the woods, way back as far as the swamps, and all the men is told not to folly'em. Boys, too. And if they's to folly'em, then they has a death curse put on'em and dies. Boy, I wouldn't want no death curse put on me. I figger I gonna die quick enough.

I couldn't believe my good luck, all this folklore and delicious gossip spilled out in a golden pool just for me, for my blank pages and pages, for my self-fueled ghost stories. Rayvon talked on.

—Somebody said them women stays out in the swamps until they get the Spirit. But I wonder if they ain't out there doing something else.

—Like what?

—I don't know. Rayvon blushed a little. Anyhow, after they been out yonder a while, they come back to the church just like he done said, everyone of 'em carrying a lit candle, and the men and the boys is waiting inside the church. And then you know what happens? Rayvon hoarsed into a whisper.

—What? I whispered back.

—Soon as they gets inside, they blows out them candles, and all hell breaks loose. All kindsa carrying-on. I heard tell. Rayvon straightened up. And that's all I know.

He took off his cap and beat it against his thigh. I don't care nothin about it no how. I done been saved eight times.

He brushed bark and sawdust off his overalls. Yeah, right down yonder at Lagoon. Rayvon packed his cap back on his head and pointed due south through the woods. And with that point, in effect, dismissing me.

When I told Clyde about this, he said, Well, no worse than the hell that breaks loose down in the group camp every summer with Mr. Creech. In fact, it sounds a lot more entertaining.

I tried to find out more about the candlewalk, looking up stuff in my dictionaries and guides to myths and symbols. Looking through *The Golden Bough*. Sir James Frazer told me lots of good things, especially about the need-fire, celebrated any time the ancient people felt a need to beg the gods for special protections against disease, vermin, blight, or a rampaging fiend. They built big bonfires, sang, danced, and prayed. Then scattered the cooled ashes in strategic places, doorsills, fields, sickbeds. But nothing Frazer described actually sounded joyful. Everything Newbold told me, everything Rayvon implied, sounded celebratory, joyful, a festival.

A day or so later, Belinda Pait, Newbold's wife, called me and said he'd told her I asked about the old-timey candlewalk.

—We don't do that, she said, in our church over in Elizabethtown. What we do is the Watch. And you always do it on New Year's Eve.

—Belinda, I said, what's it for, the Watch?

She gave a gentle, pleased sort of laugh. It's for watching out the old year and welcoming in the new. Now, this is the African Methodist Episcopal Zion, she reminded me, over in town.

I agreed. I wrote it down, telling Belinda I was raised a Methodist but we never did any candlewalks or the Watch. Actually, what I said was, We never had any fun like that.

Belinda laughed again. She confirmed the wearing of white clothes, not just for women, but also for men, and the carrying of lighted candles by both.

—Then we march around the sanctuary twice, she said, singing and praying. Some people feel the Spirit, then they preach a little bit.

Then Belinda told me something that thrilled me to the bone. She said, We don't have to wait for the New Year to do a Watch, we can do it anytime we feel a need to.

And I remembered Frazer's need-fire. And suddenly his plain text took on the color and fragrance of Bladen County, of Crusoe's Island.

I thanked Belinda for her help and put the phone back in its hard cold cradle, the receiver quite warm from my breath and skin. A candlewalk. The Watch. A need-fire.

I had lived all my life and never known these things. And that night lying in bed with Clyde and talking over the day with him, listening to the familiar sounds of the woods all around us, I drifted off to sleep thinking of the exotic Loretta and those three dark Vestals, Regina, Omega, and Elise, deep in the swamps. They stood in a little clearing festooned with Spanish moss. And they held tall white candles, each burning a tall clear flame, bright as a moon.

I watched Loretta turn and lead the way out, her pale gown foaming over her bare feet. Regina, Omega, and Elise followed and with each step, their worn old faces softened in a glory and a joy I loved.

18
Transvestite

I SAW A TELEVISION DOCUMENTARY about modern plains women living in Kansas and Nebraska. Their strong sense of isolation. Some went crazy listening to the wind blowing off the prairie. The dry whisperings of miles and miles of grass. Others just gritted their teeth and lasted it out. They developed an elaborate vocabulary to describe the color of the sky and the piling up of the clouds. A red sky meant something, a pale white something else; long hanging clouds and scudding clouds something else again. In such flat country, they could see a storm or a fire or a stranger coming for a long time. They stood outside and watched, a hand cupped over their eyes, the wind snapping at their skirts or jeans. They had patience.

All those women ever saw was the prairie grass and the wide sky. And all they heard for days, other than the voices of their husbands and children, was the wind blowing, things which changed so slowly, but so significantly.

They had harsh winters, those in which people got lost between the back door and the barn, fumbling along the deep drifts with a guide rope that froze and sank like lead. If you turned anybody away from your door in one of those killing Kansas or Nebraska winters, and if people found out you did, you could be shot. It was murder to turn a person away in the cold. To deny anybody the shelter of your roof, withhold the laying-on of warm and generous hands.

Living at Singletary Lake Group Camp was like living on the prairie. I had all the modern conveniences, every tool and comfort. I wasn't entirely cut off from the rest of the world. And neither were the plains women in the documentary. They didn't live in sod-roof cabins. They had touch-telephones and color televisions. But there was still something in the sound of the wind blowing through that grass, in those long, flat vistas that bespoke monotonous isolation.

I got up every morning and looked out the window and saw the same sort of monotony, white sand and scrub, the shallow scooping of the bays, and the crowding trees on all sides. No matter that the transmitting tower for WSOC-TV, Channel 6 Wilmington, reared 2,000 feet into my horizon, blinking its red warning lights toward aircraft, sometimes pulsing like red smears in the fog. The TV tower was something imposed upon the landscape, and far from changing the wilderness isolation, only made it more obvious.

We would stop by on our park ramblings, put our hands on the cables to feel them sway and shudder in the wind. Like putting our hands on the sinews of a giant. You could see the tower from every part of the park, but it wasn't visible on the highway until a certain bend in the long lonely road was rounded. Then the thing commanded the whole countryside, the low scrubby sand dunes and turkey oaks, and the lunar-looking pock marks that signified a bay.

Kirk at the mailbox for Singletary Lake

A naturalist from the Raleigh office told us ducks would fly into the cables, slam hard, fall to the ground, and die. We never saw any ducks doing this, either flying into the cables or lying on the ground dead.

—Maybe animals eat them? I wondered.

—Why don't other birds fly into the cables, too?

He swatted the broom straw. It's just during migrations, he guessed. It's just when big flocks of them fly over, some get confused and fly into the cables.

What did he know? He just came down there once from Raleigh on a routine park inspection. He didn't live there and look at the park every day the way we did. I saw ducks quacking and swimming on Singletary Lake the first day I got there, Christmas, 1961. Saw a great blue heron at the spillway every autumn. I'd seen Canada geese flying in a dark V every season, pulling hard through the air, right over us all. I never saw any slam into the television cables, nose dive to the ground, exploding feathers and blood across the sand.

A few miles down the road, people flew over White Lake in Piper Cubs, ten dollars a flyover. People rode the ferris wheel, the bumper cars. My own children clamored for the merry-go-round and the roller coaster. White Lake, perhaps the most beautiful of all the bay lakes, could turn into a loud summer carnival of honky-tonk neon, popcorn, Sno-Cones, and bingo. People hollered at me on the midway to come get my fortune told, get my picture taken.

The clearest water among the Carolina bays, White Lake was also the most congested, clogged with motorboats and water-skiers. In fact, such steady turbulence stirred up algae that normally clung to the bottom. The algae drifted to the surface and floated in big ugly clumps, clouding the clear water, and soon stinking in the hot sun.

People complained to Clyde, Whatcha gonna do about that stinking stuff? Gonna get rid of it?

He asked, You got a boat?

—Yeah, a big old outboard, 900 horse.

—Well, he said, get rid of that big old outboard and you'll get rid of that stinking stuff.

Every summer a few people got struck by lightning on White Lake, probably because more people stayed out on the water during a storm than on the other lakes. They'd be out there on the ends of their piers, enjoying a picnic under the pavilion, or maybe still skiing behind the big boats, shrieking and covered in clear spray, then, dead as nails.

White Lake was impressive evidence of modern civilization. And yet, like the Channel 6 television tower rearing its cables and red lights on Kelly Star Route, it often made me feel all the more isolated.

The little transvestite was certainly isolated. I first noticed him in the morning as I drove the children into Elizabethtown for some Saturday Halloween activities at the county 4-H. He was just standing by the road looking at the big lake, its cypress and Spanish moss. He'd parked his car well off the pavement, and I knew he would have a hard time later getting it out of that soft sand.

I got groceries, did errands, then picked the children up around lunch, and we drove back to the park. The man stood in the same place, still staring at the lake, his car sinking deeper into the sand. He sort of turned, as if to put himself in better profile when I passed, as if he wanted me to see him to advantage. As if he had a message.

We went home and carved pumpkins, set them on the front steps and lit candles inside. The smell of fresh pumpkin and burning wax was so comforting and homey, I didn't think any more about the stranger until Judson Glenn came for dinner. He mentioned somebody standing at the bend in the road, staring at the lake, and it getting rather dark.

I remembered, I bet that's the same guy I saw this morning.

Clyde said he hoped he wouldn't have to go pull him out in the middle of the night. We had dinner and then some long conversation. When Judson got ready to drive back toward White Lake, he promised to let Clyde know if the man was still out there.

Clyde was poking the last remnants of our fire when the phone rang.

—He's still out there, said Judson.

Clyde left to check it out. He didn't come back for hours, and I fell asleep, the fire died down to embers, and the warm dark pumpkin-scented house sailed through a mild night. Then Clyde woke me. You won't believe what happened, he said.

By the time he'd gotten to the scene, somebody had called the North Carolina Highway Patrol and the Bladen County sheriff. The man was still standing and staring at the lake. He seemed faintly delighted with the sudden attention.

The patrolmen and the sheriff and all his deputies questioned the man, but got little response. He submitted to a body search, opened his car trunk, let them paw through everything he had. They discovered women's clothes in the car. Jewelry. High-heel shoes. Make-up and perfume. Then they suspected he had murdered someone and thrown her body in Singletary Lake.

They were ready to send for a boat and drag the lake.

Then one of the deputies noticed a picture in the man's billfold. It was he, dressed in women's clothes. The patrolmen asked him to put on some of the clothes, the high-heel shoes. Everything fit. Clyde and the patrolmen realized what was going on by that time. But the sheriff and his deputies were confounded.

—A man! they said, Dressed up like a woman!

It was beyond their wildest imaginings. It was a cartoon.

The man had military papers indicating a recent discharge from Seymour Johnson Air Force Base in Wayne County, some fifty miles from the park.

The patrolmen washed their hands of the matter and left. The sheriff, however, decided to charge the man with loitering and hauled him away to spend the rest of the night in the Bladen County jail. The next day, the stranger drove off in his car full of women's clothes and jewelry and make-up, the picture of himself snug inside his billfold.

He had stood and stared at Singletary Lake all day and into Saturday night. Such a profound isolation. Brilliant cola water and pungent cypress. A bull alligator hollering on the other shore. And then those officers of the law pulling and pushing him every which way. What did he see coming toward him on the lake's horizon? What did he hear blowing through the pocosin?

Clyde and I never knew who actually got his car out of the sand. A few weeks later two fishermen brought some clothes by the park office. A dirty wet blouse and a garter belt snagged in the myrtle bushes along the lake shore.

—You reckon? I started to ask.

—Don't, Clyde held up a hand, even think it.

I went to the house, rolled paper into the Smith-Corona, and wrote a story. In the story, it is Halloween, and there are two children, like mine. The girl dresses up like Cinderella going to the ball. The boy dresses up like a sailor with a big charcoal mustache. Then the sailor falls down and cuts his chin on a piece of gravel in front of the park office. (They live in a state park called Crusoe's Island.) The little sailor bleeds a lot, ends up with a few stitches and a butterfly bandage in the county hospital emergency room.

—Bad way to spend shore leave, son, the doctor says. The little sailor's charcoal mustache is smeared with blood and candy.

—What's shore leave?

—That's when they let you go to town, dress up, and get drunk, and get a girlfriend. You got a girlfriend?

—No! says the little sailor, I'm not but in the third grade!

Back home in the state park, he and his Cinderella sister sneak off trick-or-treating and never come back. A sailor cap is found in the bushes. A pink tulle skirt floats up in the lake.

Their mother grits her teeth, Where do you think they went?

Their father holds up a hand, Don't even think it. We can't do a thing about it. Let it go.

The little transvestite, short in stature and somewhat stupefied in demeanor, nevertheless, had his effect. He was not the terror, the bad man. He was no more than a Halloween figure, perhaps, playing dress-up with a vengeance. He could be a little boy looking for some way to tame his world. He could be me. I had a sympathy for him. I recognized him. My clothing was not his. I dressed up in words, in dreams, in stories. And so I tamed my world.

He had found Singletary Lake. I had found Crusoe's Island. There was no terror. No threat in that.

So I wrote one last story to destroy the terror, or a fire bomber, or a shooter, any sort of threat happening upon me in the woods. In this story, I would see the bad man coming across the sandy yard before he saw me. I'd signal the children and we'd climb into that attic over the bathroom, pull up the disappearing stairs behind us, and then huddle there on the rafters, trying not to sneeze from the dust and the pink fiberglass insulation.

Then my story runs:

Heather and Melissa and Kirk hear him downstairs prowling each room, fingering their stuff, plates and spoons, toys, the sheets thumping in the dryer, Heather's stacks of stories beside the typewriter. Their ears follow everything. They are outraged, and helpless.

Kirk's eyes are big as saucers. Melissa's hair makes a tawny cloud in the attic gloom. And Heather is so desperately scared, she curses at them to be still, to be quiet, to please, *please!* shut up.

Kirk playing "army," 1972

After a while, the bad man is gone, and they ease back down the stairs, cry over the bodies of the slaughtered dog and two cats, the bodies of the slaughtered park rangers lying in the road, and then run to the office to see if Clyde is still alive.

Heather opens the door, the children breathing hard behind. Clyde slumps on his desk, the gray uniform shirt with the dogwood patch soaked red in blood.

—Daddy! his children cry. They rush to him, pull one big tanned arm back from his face. His eyes are still blue, still looking patiently bemused back at them.

At the end of her story, Heather, the made-up character, would have failed to keep back the terror, the bad man lurking in the dark pocosin. But that was in the story. In her reality, Heather, the writer, like the little transvestite by the lake, like all those plains women out in Kansas and Nebraska, would surely be alone but not left to her regrets. She would know what had happened. And she would know that the place she lived in was good.

And the story to write, she realizes, does not end with the man dead on his desk, the children crying. It ends with the man maybe only vanished, or with the man out there walking on water, walking across Singletary Lake with the whole world watching. Transvested. Clothed in a different dimension.

Back in their house, the woman makes a picnic, layers cheese and bologna and lettuce between bread, cuts the sandwiches on the diagonal, wraps them in waxed paper. Then she gathers the two children, the dog and the cats, and the man from the lake. They drive off together. The story is good.

19
The Good Place

I TAMED MYSELF AND MY FEARS by writing. There was no blaming the place. Regardless of what came out of its woods, Singletary Lake Group Camp was a good place. I believed I would stay there forever. But in October 1973, a committee appointed by the new governor, James Holshouser, inventoried the state park system and concluded some parks should be closed to save money. Singletary was one of those. Closing it down would save the state $26,000.

—How can they close Singletary? The children were astonished. This place was their home, the place where they slept all night, their breath clean and their heartbeat strong. *How can they close Crusoe?* My own thoughts echoed.

—It's a state park, Clyde tried to explain, They can do anything they want with it. It's not ours.

—But, Melissa and Kirk were not convinced, we live here!

Singletary Lake Group Camp wasn't just a state park to them, not just a building on an inventory. Its roof and rooms had nurtured them and made them who they were.

Clyde and I kept on explaining, trying to steer their thoughts toward other homes.

—We'll move to Badin, Clyde said. You'll have the experience of living in a little town. You'll have lots of new friends. You'll have a new school you can walk to.

—The same school Daddy and I went to, I added.

They began to warm to it slowly, especially the part about going to the same school where Clyde and I had gone. Clyde was transferred to another park, Medoc, in the northeastern part of the state, a new park as yet undeveloped. He would be expected to literally cut it out of the woods. There might be a single room for the superintendent in the park office, maybe a small trailer hook-up, but no dark pine-paneled house for the superintendent's family. No attic. No sandy yards with swings and a barbecue. No pocosin. No inland bays.

—It's like being in the Marines, he said. They tell you to go ashore, and when you get there, there's nothing to go ashore on.

—But you go, he concluded. You still go ashore.

Clyde and I couldn't go to this new park together, not yet at any rate. We would have to live apart for a while and we hated it.

—I'll get home every weekend, Clyde tried to soften the shock.

So I managed to get a teaching job at Pfeiffer College, back home in Stanly County where we got married. And even found a house in our old home town, Badin. We planned to move before Christmas. We always seemed to move at Christmas.

The children were now elated, eager for the next big adventure in their lives. They were strong people, survivors, without regret. Those woods had taught them well. They would live with me in Badin while Clyde went northeast across the state to develop the new park in Halifax County. And we would be a family again only on the weekends.

—That's the way most of the whole United States lives, Clyde pointed out, still trying to comfort us.

It was hard to take, though. I was already missing the woods, the house where I had lived for thirteen years, the place where I thought sometimes things might creep out of the pocosin and grab us. Perhaps this was what I had been dreading all that time—the actual leaving of my personal Crusoe.

Kirk gave away most all of his playthings to Ivory McCoy's little boys. They congregated one day and received with gracious surprise the soccer ball, the basketball, the Tonka trucks, the pogo stick. Melissa went for a final slumber party with girls from Bladen Elementary. The children's minds were made up. Singletary Lake Group Camp already a polished relic for them.

It struck me we all might be about to reinvent ourselves, about to enter alien dimensions. Might never again come home to something so simple and so secret as these woods. And this time it was not heralded by swarms of lightning bugs festooning a hot June night the way they had thirteen years before.

I thought how Melissa had used to mark out special places— *Look, this is Silk Afternoon. That down there in the bushes is Bad Dream*—marking each feature of Crusoe's Island as her own. Mapping her existence by tree and path, matching each natural thing to some significant feature of her own life—an emotion or a dream or an experience. The events of children. And as he grew up beside her, she had taught them to Kirk.

Soon everything Melissa, and also Kirk, knew would belong to other people. Everything Melissa had marked upon her own special map would be lost. Nobody would know—except, maybe, in my story.

And Melissa herself might forget. The landmarks of my children, I promised, must be saved in some fashion. The mark of

The Easter egg hunt, Lagoon Baptist Church, 1964

existence, my and Clyde's and Melissa's and Kirk's, might, indeed, have to be salvaged.

Yet, and again, yet—Singletary Lake Group Camp was not ours.

Perhaps existence itself was not even ours. Just a time borrowed for awhile, so short, and so what to do with it, what?

I made my own peace by burning letters, every letter Clyde and I had written to each other from the time we first dated at Morrow Mountain State Park, throughout my finishing college in Greensboro, and whatever had passed between us since. I'd kept them all in a small trunk that once belonged to old Grandmother Martha Anna Smith, the one who dipped snuff and ate poke salad in the spring. It was her wedding trunk, with a curved and hinged lid, a faded calico lining, and a sharp broken lock. I kept other things in there, too, the children's baby clothes, my baby clothes, a little white embroidered coat Clyde's mother made—*He was walking when I made that*, she told me.

I leafed through all the letters, faded stacks of legal-size envelopes, fingered the different addresses, Albemarle, Greensboro, Elizabethtown. And then, without reading a single one—I just didn't want to look at those long-gone and much loved lives again—I burned them in the fireplace. The smoke rose up the chimney as the fire licked each one, curled its long edges, and devoured it. I knew someday my children would ask me why I did this.

I wondered, as the pages shuddered into ash, at the things I might tell them. Melissa and Kirk, the true heirs of the burning. And if they would believe me.

In late November, right after Thanksgiving, the weather was warm and cloudy-bright, up to eighty degrees for three days, unbelievable weather. Clyde and I slept with the windows open all night and listened to the cicadas hollering in the grass outside. We lay close to each other, the sheets cool over us, the air mild as spring. Clyde murmured how he liked lying there, hearing the cicadas through the window. I pulled even closer, trying in my half-sleep to pull what was left of Crusoe's Island also closer to us. All night I dreamed of my grandmothers, Martha Anna Smith and Jennie Ross, long dead these years:

In my dream, they are sweeping front porches, hanging bunches of herbs to dry in sunny kitchens, cutting out soft little dresses to sew for babies. One of them, I cannot tell which, cuts her hand, bleeds. The other one goes outdoors to the huge fig bush flourishing next to the house, pulls a choice ripe fig, and returns to squeeze the milky fig juice over the bleeding hand. She explains the ripe fig will stop the blood, heal the wound. It will hold tight, she says, now it will cling and heal. The sweet fig drips through her fingers, the little dark seeds freckling her knuckles. And the fig bush flutters its leaves that look like big turkey feet all over my dream with a sound like the cicadas hollering at Crusoe.

Dry turkey oak leaves, the same shape as old fig bush leaves, fluttered in the balmy air when Clyde and I walked next morning to the spillway, crossed over the dam, and went up the white sandy road. Tomorrow would be colder, though still bright and windy, with some late showers. The turkey oaks would be stripped clean.

But that day the wind made everything crisp and summer-like. We climbed through a big pond bay thicket that opened out like a high room, the branches stretching together over our heads. Brown leaves and pine needles softened the ground. We decided to celebrate a festival in there, something for the place to remember us by, so we made love out in the open, you might say, with the woods watching, applauding.

Afterward, I felt content, as if sitting in my porch swing and listening to the unseasonably warm wind worrying the bamboo chimes that dangled from the eaves. A moment of delight and abandon, a moment of high surprise. A turning point.

Just like the Thanksgiving cactus back in my kitchen loaded with ripe red buds, soon I might bloom. *Glory.*

Clyde said to leave something behind, something for people to find and wonder about. So we draped our underwear on the pond bay branches.

—That'll surprise 'em.

I was coming down Kelly Star Route in the Beetle about five miles before the turn into the park, and I saw a tall woman striding along the sandy shoulder. Her stride steady and proud, her head forward, it was unmistakably the impressive Loretta. I slowed down, lowered the window, You want a ride?

Loretta turned only a little to look at me, never slacking her pace as I drove along beside. Then she halted, opened the door, and settled herself into the bucket seat. I felt embarrassed for a woman so spectacular as Loretta to have to sit in a bucket seat. We rode in silence, Loretta gazing straight ahead.

—I need me one of them cigarettes, she said. The only words she'd ever spoken to me. I'd been living in those woods thirteen years, seeing Loretta and Ivory nearly every week, and those were our first words. That was also the first time I'd ever seen Loretta walking on the side of the road. She had nothing with her, no pocketbooks or bundles, no children.

I shook a cigarette from the open pack and Loretta accepted, pushed in the car's lighter, settled back again with such obvious pleasure, I was pleased to be a part of it. Loretta inhaled deeply, letting the smoke, startlingly white against her bronze freckled skin, tumble back out her nose. She never said another thing.

At the turn into the park, I slowed, let the car idle, and Loretta got out, still dragging on the cigarette, and strode across Kelly Star Route, past the big mailbox, vanishing into the turkey oaks.

I wanted to holler something at her. Wanted to tell Loretta to come back and get all the cigarettes. I wanted her to know I was leaving the woods before Christmas with my husband and my two children.

But I didn't do it. I accelerated into the turn and drove to the dark, paneled house. The smell of Loretta, rich and fruity, a smell beyond language or symbol, climbed out of the car with me, and I wore it long past supper, long past sleeping.

And right before sleeping, Clyde and I lay talking in our old familiar habit, talking and listening to the night outside, the sounds and sources of Crusoe's Island, the ancient speech of wilderness. Then we slept, thinking just before genuine darkness fell upon us, We may never sleep this way again, in this place, with these sounds.

Then darkness.

The recommendations of the state committee were not taken, and Singletary Lake Group Camp survived to be expanded and developed into several more camping areas, hiking trails, and boating facilities. It would be a different park someday, open year-round for big groups of campers, and well-used.

Clyde and I were glad. We would hate to see it closed, the campgrounds falling to ruin, the house cold and empty, the lake silting into peat. And though the children were relieved, already their faces and minds had turned toward the new life they would have somewhere else.

—People will still live here, Kirk patted the fireplace.

Clyde nodded, They'll have good times.

—And the same woods will be here, too, Melissa looked across the sandy yard. Suddenly the dog dashed into a pile of pine cones, nosed one up, and barked.

The children were right, the fireplace, the woods, the lake would all survive as they must, as they do. And the Millers survived, leaving Singletary Lake Group Camp in December 1973, another Christmas, going deliberately.

But I remembered it the way we left it, the moonlight and the animals, the bone-white sand, the glossy cola water, a man and woman and two children. This way:

Poochie sleeps covered in dry leaves, groaning awake, stretching and wagging his tail. When we walk to the lake, he suddenly strikes a deer trail. The doe plunges into the water and Poochie, fool dog, thinks he can catch her, swimming in big clumsy dives, up and down under, back up. The doe leaves him behind and comes out so far on the other side, we can barely pick out her shape. Poochie looks bewildered, returns to the shore and shakes himself off.

There are old turpentine cuts on the big pines. And in a small cypress bay, patches of broom straw so red, they seem to glow in the late sun. The children gather their arms full, say they're going to make me some brooms.

Back in the house, the rooms are cozy and warm and smell like the gingerbread I chopped apples into before I baked it. There is a Thanksgiving cactus rooting in a glass of water on the kitchen sill, gourds and pumpkins all over the table, and on the front porch, deer antlers rise like branches of candles.

At night, after the moon rises, after the fire dies, a cricket sings somewhere in the house, I can't tell where. When I get up and look, he stops just as I get too close, then starts up again as I go away. The wind blows leaves over the sand, dry, skittish. The geoasters curl open out there, the yellow ipecac shrivels, and somewhere snow is blowing toward us.

In the morning, I spread out my notebooks and write this.

20
Epilogue: Blue Moon

EVERYTHING IN BADIN A SMOKY DREAM. Down the hill, across the glow of Badin Lake, the aluminum smelter rumbled and spilled off pure metal. Sodium vapor street lights softened Elm Street's houses and quiet yards. I woke up on the north side of our house, pulled air deep into myself, relieved to be alive, then stirred around getting dressed in Kirk's old room. The relics and totems of a grown child's life amused and heartened me: his glamorous California surfing posters, the track trophies, his dignified Eagle medal hanging from the lamp, and a big shabby community of teddy bears, Tasmanian devils, and sock monkeys sprawled over the spare bunk.

When I came through the laundry room, I saw, framed in the little window over the Whirlpool washer, a herd of brown deer. They stretched in shadows around the dark wet hickories of the back yard, browsed the February leaves, nosing for crocuses, hyacinths, any new shoots starting up.

I counted nine deer, all doe, and admired their grace and caution. I leaned on the slick cold machine to drink them in, and I knew it wasn't a vision everybody got to see. I wanted to hold them in my mind and carry them around like amber jewels, rubbing that amber to strike off bright sparks. Nine deer. Now fading across the yard. A moment given to me for respite. For all the time on the other side of the house, Clyde was dying.

December 1990 was the blue moon, the time when two full moons are seen in the same thirty days. Seven times every nineteen years, two full moons appear the same month. Last happened in May 1988, and would happen again in August 1993. The folklore of the blue moon fascinated me. The right mixture of beauty and peril, all that old spicy allure of Crusoe's Island, a time when we lived right on the edge.

In 1990, it had been exactly nineteen years since the last blue moon shone on a New Year's Eve. And on New Year's Eve, the full moon radiant, Clyde went into surgery and was found to have advanced pancreatic cancer already spread to the liver, no chance, no hope, nothing left to do, and nothing to look forward to.

My mind closed down when I heard the word. The surgeon stood in the hospital lounge, his green scrubs rumpled and his cap pushed to the back of his head.

—We found cancer in there. And then he said other things like, a tumor covering the distal end of the pancreas. We removed the spleen, advanced necrosis.

I heard Melissa ask questions like transplant? how many years? The surgeon hurried to say not years, not years, maybe months. The lounge was full of people sitting and waiting, drinking plastic cups of Coca-Cola and Pepsi, flipping magazines. It didn't seem as if Clyde could be lying somewhere in such a place cut open, stapled back together, and given up to die.

I determined he would not die. This month of the blue moon surely counted. So many things had happened to us before in those years in the park, years when we only had each other, and we survived. We'd witnessed other cosmic events there, and each time our life got stronger, more resonant. This blue moon would be the same. There'd be no dying. I had proof:

Somewhere in those state park years, a rainbow pulled from horizon to horizon over the coastal plateau outside Fayetteville, the south side of Cumberland County toward Bladen. Clyde drove our Karmann Ghia right through it, rain on one side, hot sun on the other, the two children marveling in the tiny black-leathered rumble seat. We were on the way to Shakey's for pizza and sarsaparillas and old movies. The brilliant colors of that big rainbow arching through the stormy sky were forever remembered with the taste and smell of oregano and wood smoke, yeast and dark sugar syrup. The taste and smell of a family in love with itself.

In March 1970, Clyde and I watched the total eclipse of the sun, our ordinary noontime going dark, the temperature dropping, and a strong wind suddenly sweeping through the park trees. We were in the path of totality three minutes. Out in the swamps, foxes ran in circles, black bears went to sleep, and alligators bellowed. All nature seemed disturbed. Then the sun came back and roosters crowed across the highway in Ivory McCoy's yard. Clyde and I took back our old life.

Then we were transferred away from Singletary Lake Group Camp. Clyde went to another park. The children and I went back to Badin because there was no residence for us at the new and undeveloped park. And now under a blue moon, nature was disturbed again by this vicious illness, an invader in the night, another terror. Surely Clyde and I would wake up and take back our old life again. But we were a long way from Crusoe's Island, from Ivory McCoy, from Kirk sitting in the sun and all those old remedies. I heard the sounds of Melissa crying, felt her arms around me. And in a little while, I went to a phone to call Kirk. Not years, the surgeon said, not years.

The years sprang back to me, in memories, in stories. Like that long ago surprise afternoon shower in Bladen County, when I sat on the porch with the children. And I watched a big piece of black plastic flap in the wind. I first thought it was a big black dog, frolicking at the edge of the woods, maybe at the end of his leash, maybe put there by a park patron now inside the office talking with Clyde.

The black dog leaped up and darted down so full of life. And so silent. Then I saw it was plastic. A piece of a garbage bag, those that lined the big cans set around the park for public use. Black and silent. Bright in the flashings of the shower. But I kept on watching, still on the chance it might be alive, might really be that dog I first noticed.

No dog. Then I watched a bit longer, rocking as the children talked and played. And stories fell into place. Things I promised I'd remember to write down for the children when the shower was over and everything full of the wonderful washed smell rising off the woods and the sand.

Things like:

One time Clyde and I drove hard back from Greensboro where I was still in school. We wanted to get down to Morrow Mountain. We could have the whole weekend alone in the barracks. Just Clyde and me.

But it rained, threw quick and flashing hard little showers all the way down 49, the long blacktop glistening bright as sucked candy. I sat closer to Clyde, gathering in his smell and his warmth.

It wasn't cold, but it seemed cold, the glistening black road and the explosions of rain. I looked off into a patch of woods, dark trees crowded close as toothpicks, a creek running to the brim with fresh rain, the faint bubbling sshh as we shot over the low bridge.

And I had a vision of me, and Clyde running after me, through the rainy crowded woods. I could feel the showers all over me. I could even feel, I thought, the showers all over him.

—Clyde, I said, would you go chase after me in the woods in the rain? Would you go run me down and bring me back?

—What woods? he said.

—Woods, I insisted. Just woods.

Clyde considered this a moment. The wipers scrubbed at the old gray Plymouth and there echoed a deep thud of thunder somewhere off to the back of us. Clyde grinned and pulled me closer than I already was. I would, he agreed. You know I would.

And:

I don't believe anybody's named Clyde, I said when we first met, down in the park at Morrow Mountain one hot Sunday. Clyde was policing traffic and stopped me in the right lane coming down from the top of the mountain. A heavy stream of cars, everybody hot and impatient, air-conditioning kicking off, kids yelling out windows. I read the name off his ranger's badge.

—What do you believe they're named? He smelled of sweat and soap and some wild scent, like crushed green leaves, grapevines, pine needles.

I didn't have an answer, just blinked and flirted and drove on when he let me. Later, when I went to work in the park office, we sparred and flirted and eventually went out.

—Clyde? my parents asked, Clyde Miller? Who's Clyde Miller? What do you mean going out with somebody like that? He's too old for you.

I couldn't stand living with them. But I was stuck right then, as all girls are stuck. Not finished with school, hanging on to a summer job, driving my father's car. I knew my parents were not bad. Just aggravating. Still, I could not stand them. Years later, of course, I saw things a bit differently. Years later I wondered that my parents could stand me, the sassy and indifferent teenager I was.

Back then, I liked to do what I called feeding my eyes. From earliest memory. Such as looking a long, lazy time at a yard full of fresh white clover blooms loaded with honeybees. I would feed my eyes on the bright green and the scattered white, the frowzy hummings of the bees. And I liked to watch the lights and darks of this view change as the time of day changed, or as wind scattered through the trees and rearranged the clover and the bees beneath.

Or I fed my eyes on the night sky in winter, bitter cold, so cold it stiffened the little hairs of your nose. And stars, fine as cornmeal, dusted the sky. I stood out on the back porch of our Badin apartment and gazed and fed until my face got numb. Until my mother, searching and calling up and downstairs, saw me and made me come in.

And so when I met Clyde, at nineteen, I began feeding my eyes on him. He'd say, Hey, what're you looking at?

I'd say, At you.

He laughed. And put his big hand over my eyes so I had to shut them. Then I fed my eyes, shut tight, on Clyde's hand, as cozy blurry images danced there, dark red, as burning and thrilling as dark water.

And these are the relics I had to remember. And the urge to write them all down and salvage them was as strong as those many years ago when I came out of the stories on the porch at Singletary Lake Group Camp. Melissa and Kirk were clamoring for something. We want to run out in the rain, Mama! We want to run out and get rained on!

—Okay, I agreed, okay, and watched them rush outside, stamping in the bright puddles, turning their faces up and licking at the drops. They ran right through that piece of black plastic over near the shop, stamped it flat, and ran on.

So it was the story of such relics I knew I must tell. And how the story unfolds, then refolds itself, covers itself up and shakes itself free, maybe like a good old dog, old Poochie at Singletary, rising from his bed of brown leaves in the morning. The promise of the rising, the promise of the morning.

One thing Clyde appeared to like was the sight and smell of fresh laundry. I dumped baskets on the bed around him, shirts and towels still warm from the dryer, fragrant as a harvest. I took my time sorting and folding, all the time talking to Clyde, telling him things about the shirts and towels.

—You remember this? I held up his old uniform shirt, shook out the long gray sleeves. He'd never thrown a single one of them away, just removed the official patches and kept wearing them.

—From the park. I took the patch off. See?

I talked to him, urging and prompting, encouraging something, anything, I didn't know what. He had closed himself off, what the hospice people told me would happen. A way of dealing with the shock, the hard edge, the closing in of the dark. Each day another door shut.

I ran my fingers over the darker gray fabric where the state park patch used to be stitched. The rest of the shirt was a pewter gray, the cotton tough as nails. It had lasted these years. It would outlast the man.

Clyde blinked at me. Maybe it was too much, the knowledge of a sure and swiftly approaching death. He wouldn't speak. But the gray shirt smelled sweet and still felt warm and I shook it out again, spread it over his chest, fitting it to his neck, everything backwards, the long sleeves fluttering like flags.

—You remember? I urged, You remember Singletary?

I wanted him to remember. To retrieve every crumb and particle of the old story. To reassemble our old life, get up out of his bed and walk. I wanted him to stomp around this house as he had once in Bladen County in that house of dark pine panels, coughing and sneezing, brewing strong aromatic coffee, embracing plain life. I wanted him to do it right now, right in the middle of his cancer, his pain, the very teeth of his death. Do it, Clyde, I willed, balling a fist, remember.

He watched me, the eyes so blue and the face so smooth, such a passive beauty upon him, I couldn't believe he was really sick and dying in front of me. I took his hand and rubbed each finger, hard and squared off at the tip, the same hand Kirk inherited.

—Clyde, I said, you remember?

Finally, something. He stirred to take a deep breath, pat the shirt, pat my hand, and said gently, You tell me. Tell me again.

As much as I would ever be given.

You tell me. Tell me again.

And I put these relics together, wrote them all out, sometimes sitting on the bed beside Clyde sleeping there as soundly as my children used to sleep at Singletary. I moved my Macintosh into that room and typed the pages. Clyde would wake and look at me, much as Kirk used to look at me from the wicker carriage when I pounded out my first stories on the old Royal.

Then the pages were ready and I gave them to Clyde and he read every word, the last words of mine he ever read. And he made little changes.

—You know, it was helicopters, not airplanes the paratroopers jumped from. Clyde smiled quietly at me, turned a page.

—And Kirk didn't see Wilbur get hit by that motorcycle. He heard it.

These were things I had gotten wrong, misremembered somehow. I was delighted he remembered them right. And I made the changes there as he pointed them out on the pages. It was a good moment, warm and fresh. We traded memories. We stored them against the future

So that February morning, as I watched the brown deer so early and so promising, Clyde was still on the other side of the house dying. When the last of the nine deer faded away and the sun burned through the mist, filling the back yard with harsh reflections, I crammed everything I could find into the washer. Shirts, towels, and sneakers, piles of tame domestic things that couldn't hurt or fight back. They would churn around and thump against the drum and make noise and comfort me. I wanted the noise, the good old common thumpings and sloshings. The water rushed to fill the machine, and I added soap, softener, anything to make life smell good again, anything to harvest health and promise. Anything to return Clyde to me, and to him, another blue moon, seven times over, seven times over.

Why not why not why not?

Anger and death do not end my story, the story started so long ago on the slant-top desk, typewriter sliding down with each page. Loss does not erase my memory of Melissa and Kirk and Clyde Miller. The park taught us too much of health and good humor and stubborn love. The children and I never lost the adventure of Crusoe's Island any more than we lost Clyde. He had gone to other parks and developed them, Medoc Mountain, Raven Rock, while the children and I stayed in the small aluminum-smelting town, Badin. Clyde retired from the park system in June 1984. We planned many celebrations and adventures together, especially to go back to Singletary Lake Group Camp for one more picnic, a kind of homecoming. Clyde said maybe our underwear was still down there hanging on the pond bay.

Then the invasion I so long feared those early years came to take him. The bad thing took him, not me. Not at Singletary, but in Badin. But he did read the memories I wrote for him. And he saw in them just how good a place Singletary Lake Group Camp had been for us all. Although he never talked about it, Clyde had always felt he'd done me some kind of injustice marrying me and taking me off to live thirteen years in the woods, alone with two babies. But the books came as easily as the babies. The stories. The rememberings. No other place would have given such goodness to me. I was so glad he now knew that. And that I raised it all up from the dead, my last gift to Clyde.

He fought off death one month, two, making it through January and February as the seasons changed and the blood-red camellias bloomed outside the windows. As the days slipped into March, Clyde slept most of the time and when he was awake, his mind had already drifted toward new dimensions. The people from hospice came and sat with him so I could go out for a walk or get groceries.

And so it happened that eighteen years later, in the middle of downtown Albemarle, three hours inland from the coastal park where that lone pigeon came to us, I discovered a colony of similar pigeons roosting in a derelict building, what used to be the old Raylass Department Store. Kirk had been browsing the windows of a pawnshop looking for a splash cymbal. I was just browsing the windows of the old Raylass, looking for nothing, but remembering a lot of things, shoring up my energy to go back home to Clyde.

I peered into the thick gloom, noticing the shafts of sunlight falling from holes in the roof. Then I saw a pair of wings, then another, a flutter of pale feathers, then a whole rafter full of pigeons came into view as my eyes adjusted to the shadows.

They sat there like bouquets pinned to their roost. Some flew from one perch to another over the old Raylass aisles. I remembered shopping there, the racks of foamy prom dresses, their pale tulle billowing against the glass. The faux leather jackets in impossible aquas and tangerines. Piles of shoes, our favorite black ballerinas and penny loafers.

And now all these pigeons. The Raylass Store was open to the sky, and the pigeons had it.

When Kirk came over, I said, Look in there and wait a minute and tell me what you see.

He cupped his eyes and looked in. Then acknowledged, Oh, pigeons.

He looked at me with wise old eyes in the middle of a strong young face. Yes, he said, a smile spilling right over into his ears, pigeons. And I knew he never had forgotten, never would forget those pigeons down at Singletary, at the Capitol in Raleigh. The stories had taken deep root, risen up tall, and flourished.

And so we went home to Clyde, still sleeping, the red camellias dropping petals against the windowpane. It was Saturday. The next morning, Sunday, March 3, 1991, Clyde died. The day began with a heavy fog, then progressed to some of the hardest driving rain I'd ever seen, splashing and pouring all over, as if somebody threw buckets at the house.

The next week under a snapping blue sky, we are skimming along the back roads of New Hanover and Columbus and Bladen, skimming through alternate patches of sun and shadow, Kirk driving, Melissa navigating. I sit and ride and listen, a plain cardboard box in my lap. The box measures nine and a fourth inches by seven and a fourth, weighs about five pounds, and contains Clyde's ashes. The four of us going back to Singletary Lake Group Camp. Houses still stand in white sand edged by trees trailing heavy Spanish moss, rich as braided hair. And I remember driving these back roads with Clyde on park patrol, finding old Regina, Omega, and Elise, their fires and folk wisdom, a baby asleep in my lap, *Boys you treats as mean as you likes. But when it comes to lovin, ain't nothin like a girl.*

I really expect to see Ivory McCoy and the enigmatic Loretta, still crowned by her magnificent dreadlocks, and Tyrone, turned now into a tall weathered man at their side, taller and more enigmatic, perhaps than either parent. I expect them to step through

Clyde Miller

the red broom straw and stand like three dark Figures welcoming me back.

I recognize trees, outbuildings, blueberry bogs and bee hives, the big Channel TV transmitter sparkling against the sun. Kirk wants to approach Singletary by this route, entering Kelly Star Route cross-country rather than coming from Elizabethtown.

—It's the way Daddy used to take us to the beach, says Melissa, the way we always went. Racing through the backwoods, straight to the sea!

Except now we are racing straight inland, over white sand and scrub, the turkey oaks, the junipers festooned in gray moss, the occasional glint of brilliant cola-dark water in the sun.

And finally through the alternate sun and shadow, through the dazzling sand and woods, there is the redwood sign, the gate announcing Singletary Lake Group Camp, the familiar breathless mystery of Crusoe's Island, and for one sudden and surprisingly clear moment, we are back home.

And somewhere in the shimmering fragrant horizon heavy with pine and pond bay, the faint splash of dark water underneath, Clyde asks me again, Can you stand this, can you live this?

We find our way through the tunnel and out onto the long pier, the air like honey, clear and healthy and young. At the end of the pier, we bend around the box. Kirk says we each sprinkle two big silver spoonsful until the ashes are gone.

Melissa goes first. The ashes are colorful, pink and creamy as shells, with startling bits of carbon rolling among them, and gritty, not like the fine dust I'd expected. These are pure elements. What remains of Clyde.

The ashes drop into the water, glint bright as gold in the sun, turn once, then settle gently toward the dark lake bottom, still catching the sun, drifting and turning. It's like music, long graceful music, with no words. I am at peace with this sight, my husband of thirty-one years, thirteen of them lived beside this lake, my husband drifting and settling golden in the late afternoon sun.

We put him in the water that spreads toward the junipers, the thick wild blueberry bogs. When we are finished, Kirk throws the silver spoon and it spirals end over end toward the center of Singletary. The spoon splashes down and we hug together while the wind and the water snap around us and the sun lights up the junipers and everything feels clean.

HEATHER ROSS MILLER is the author of fifteen books, including collections of short stories and poems, and novels. She received the Alumni Distinguished Achievement Award from her alma mater, the University of North Carolina at Greensboro, and also the North Carolina Award for Literature, one of the highest honors her native state bestows. She currently teaches creative writing and literature at Washington and Lee University in Lexington, Virginia, where she is the Thomas H. Broadus, Jr., Professor of English.

OTHER SERIES BY COASTAL CAROLINA PRESS

CAROLINA YOUNG PEOPLE
Pale As the Moon—Donna Campbell
Sink or Swim: African-American Lifesavers of the Outer Banks
   —Carole Boston Weatherford

CAROLINA CLASSICS, A REPRINT SERIES
Sweet Beulah Land—Bernice Kelly Harris
The Ballad of the Flim-Flam Man—Guy Owen

LIFESTYLE SERIES
Creating a Beautiful Landscape—Henry Rehder

ENVIRONMENTAL SERIES
Eye of the Storm: Essays in the Aftermath—Ellen Rickert, editor
Troubled Waters: The Floods of '99—Andy Scott, illustrated by
   B. Case
North Carolina State Parks in the Coastal Plain: A Video
   Produced by Environmental Media, Inc.

CAROLINA VOICES SERIES
A Raising Up: Memories of a North Carolina Childhood
   —R. C. Fowler

SEASCAPE SERIES, PRESENTED BY THE NORTH CAROLINA
   MARITIME MUSEUM
Voyage of the Paper Canoe—Nathaniel Bishop

AUDIO BOOKS
Sink or Swim—**An Audio Dramatization**
   Produced by Ziplow Productions, Inc.
Pale As the Moon—**Single Reader**
   Produced by Masonboro Sound

10/00

E
Miller
Miller
Crusoe's Island